D1236905

MEXICO IN A NUTSHELL

AND OTHER ESSAYS

University of California Press | Berkeley and Los Angeles

1964

MEXICO IN A NUTSHELL

AND OTHER ESSAYS

ALFONSO REYES—AMBASSADOR TO BRAZIL
From a caricature in Caras y Caretas

ALFONSO REYES

Translated by Charles Ramsdell
with a foreword
by Arturo Torres-Rioseco

University of California Press
Berkeley and Los Angeles
California

Cambridge University Press
London, England

© *1964 by*
The Regents of the University of California
Library of Congress Catalog Card No. 64-21776

Published with the Assistance of a Grant from the
Rockefeller Foundation

Printed in the United States of America

Contents

Diogenes of Anáhuac

ALFONSO REYES died in 1959.

I met him ten years before his death, and I visited him almost every year during that decade. The most vivid remembrance of those visits is probably the first. One afternoon, José Gaos, the Spanish philosopher, told me: "Alfonso is sick in bed. He wishes you to call on him, although he sees very few people."

Gaos and I went together to the home of the Master, in General Benjamín Hill, 122. Alfonso was lying in bed, in his magic library. He was surrounded by books, magazines, letters, and newspapers. There were books all over the room: on bookshelves, on tables and chairs, under the pillows and blankets, on the floor. It seemed that his round, small body was an island submerged in a sea of books.

What a strange sensation of roundness and lightness! Alfonso begins to talk. His movements betray his emotion. If we had not appeared at five o'clock that afternoon he might have died. All his life is expression: he has to give everything: ideas, feelings, remembrances. He speaks and smiles, smiles with his restless eyes, with his bald head, with his moustache, with his short arms. As one day he traveled from city to city and from country to country, now he goes from book to book, from theme to theme, from anecdote to anecdote. His intelligence pours out of the dimples in his cheeks, out of his mouth and his eyes.

We think of a rubber ball bouncing over an uneven surface, stopping and moving again. We know that Alfonso is a prisoner in his bed and in his library, and yet we look up to the transparent air, where the intellectual acrobat is pirouetting.

While I was conversing with Alfonso I had to sharpen my eyes, I had to follow the little ball in its race and its jumps because if you lose sight of it you may lose a precious reference to Dante, to Góngora, or Mallarmé. The scholars of the future will count the quotations from Cervantes or Plato in his books, but, alas! nobody will ever know how many times Reyes quoted his masters in his conversations.

Gaos returns from his excursion through the shelves, and Alfonso exclaims:

"We have had fifteen minutes of delightful conversation."

Gaos says, "We have been here two hours and it is time to let the patient rest."

Before departing I ask Alfonso if he has all my books in his library.

"I believe I have them," says Alfonso, "Look for yourself."

I look, but find only one.

"There are others," exclaims Reyes. "Somebody has taken them."

"Yes," I retort, "Frestón* the magician, my enemy."

The little ball of intelligence and grace is inflated and bursts into loud laughter.

My last meeting with Reyes took place a few months before his death (August 10, 1959). It was a clear August morning. Since I was too early for the visit I decided to walk around and look at the neighborhood. I lost my way and I asked several people:

"Where is the home of Don Alfonso Reyes?"

Nobody knew who Don Alfonso Reyes was, a fact that is more symbolic of our times than of Mexico.

Alfonso was a changed man. He was as kind and as mentally alert as ever, but physically weak. He had retired to his home and did not leave his library, though he wrote two articles daily, for the newspapers, and knew well what was happening in the intellectual world in Mexico City as well as in Madrid or Paris.

---

* Reyes has written a story about Frestón, the magician who hid the books in *Don Quijote*.

"In Mexico," he told me, "the young writers spend too much time in cocktail parties and polemics. They believe that culture can be gotten out of thin air." He had read all the latest books of his compatriots, but he preferred his dialogues with Plato and his monologues with Unamuno.

I asked him about his work.

"I am finishing up my final editions," he said. "But still I have to work on my correspondence, and my Memoirs are not yet completed."

The Master was tired that day. Bearded and bald, round-bellied, he looked like an old Buddha in his armchair. He was leaning on a cane. When I said good-by to him I had to help him up. We embraced for the last time; I descended the stairs of his library and waved at him from the ground floor. There he stood head down, perhaps hiding a tear, this great man, born in the wrong age and in the wrong country . . . for Reyes was essentially a humanist.

Those who knew Reyes as a young man speak of his small body and his large head, of his moustache and his eternal pipe, of his smile and his sensitive hands. They also noticed his eyes, warm with intelligence and understanding. The most noble words of the language have been used in describing his personality. His younger friends remember the simplicity of his affection; his disciples remember his kind words of guidance, the imperceptible advice. They all admired his kindness to the young men who were beginning their literary careers.

"Cortesía" is the word most often used—"cortesía," which means good manners, refinement, gentleness, rather than courtesy. "Cortesía" is considered to be a typical Mexican characteristic; it is almost a synonym of loving friendship. "When Reyes was twenty-four years old, in Madrid, he knew how to smile, talk and listen," says one of his Spanish friends. He had the proverbial humility of the scholar, the charm of the "raconteur," the tolerance of the wise. He was quick in gesture and word, but never impatient or impetuous, and the fire of his dialogue was always tempered by the softness of his smile.

He was in love with "the word," both in speech and in writing. To use the precise and elegant word was also a point of "cortesía" toward the language. His brain was a rich source of ideas, theories, and fantasies; these he expressed, out of respect for reader and listener, in a clear and logical manner: another form of "cortesía." All his opinions were based on perfect knowledge of the subject being discussed. He never talked for the mere sake of talking, this modern humanist of Mexico.

Reyes was born in Monterrey in May, 1889. His father was a general in Porfírio Díaz's army. He went to primary and second-ary schools in his native city. In 1905 he attended the Escuela Nacional Preparatoria in Mexico City and later the Escuela Nacional de Altos Estudios. He obtained his law degree in 1913 and then taught the history of the Spanish language and literature for only a brief period, for this same year he was appointed Second Secretary of the Mexican Legation in Paris.

Reyes was not satisfied with being only a university student. He became a friend of his professors and of the well-known writers of his time. He was the youngest member of the Generation of the Centenary, a cosmopolitan group of essayists and philosophers including José Vasconcelos, Pedro Henríquez Ureña, and Antonio Caso. These writers founded the Ateneo de la Juventud (1909), an institution that had a great impact on the approaching Mexican renaissance. Henríquez, Vasconcelos, Reyes, and above all, Antonio Caso put an end to positivism, the reigning philosophy of the previous era.

Reyes was the only member of the Ateneo who had, besides the cult of classic knowledge, a great devotion for Spanish, Mexican, and Spanish American literature; hence his studies on Góngora, Othón and his essay on landscape in nineteenth-century poetry.

Reyes was in Paris only one year. The European war of 1914 and the suppression of the Mexican diplomatic service made it impossible for him to remain in France.

He went to Spain the same year. He was extremely poor and had the responsibility of caring for a wife (Manuelita) and a two-year-old baby. He had difficult days in Madrid, but soon he was living a most active and full life in the Spanish capital. He translated books, became secretary of the Madrid Ateneo, and finally was given a position in the Centro de Estudios Históricos.

In five years he had become a "madrileño," a friend of the outstanding writers (Azorín, Jiménez, Unamuno, Azaña, Ortega, Diez Canedo), a columnist for the most important papers of the capital, *El Imparcial* and *El Sol*, and a young intellectual of promise.

In 1920—the political situation having improved in Mexico— he was recalled to his legation in Madrid. From 1924 to 1927 Reyes was Minister of Mexico in France; from 1927 to 1930 he was appointed Ambassador to Argentina; from 1930 to 1935, Ambassador to Brasil: from this year until 1939, when he returned to Mexico, Reyes was sent on very important missions to both countries.

On returning to his native land Reyes devoted his time and energies to literary work and education. He founded the Colegio de México and the Colegio Nacional; he taught in the university; he lectured in state universities; he wrote for the national journals, but above all, he began to prepare and publish his complete works.

He was writing his last article on the eve of his death.

His death closed a cultural epoch: all the intellectual men of the revolutionary era were now gone: Caso, Henríquez, Ureña, José Vasconcelos, as well as the great artists, José Clemente Orozco and Diego Rivera.

Alfonso Reyes will remain in the history of Hispanic literatures mainly as an essay writer. He is, perhaps, only a popularizer of scientific principles, a commentator on history, a definer and a systematizer. But, of course, in our America these are noble activities. Strict disciplines hold him firm at the roots of all problems discussed, and his logical mind establishes a rational balance between fact and fancy. He is always elegant and imaginative, evanescent and logical. In the selections presented in the present book, especially on America's themes and Columbus's ventures, one does not know whether to admire more the factual interpretation or the ironic sequences of the author.

In his first important book of literary essays, *Cuestiones estéticas* (1916), Reyes reveals an unusual knowledge of classic and modern European literatures and at the same time of literary theories from the Aristotelian system to contemporary techniques.

Studying the poetry of Góngora and Mallarmé, he defends the right of the poet to create his own vocabulary according to the needs of his inspiration, and argues that the world of these two poets could not have been translated into poetic experience except by the creation of a new language. Later on, during his residence in Spain, Reyes wrote some of his best essays, which were collected later in his books *Cuestiones Gongorinas* and *Capítulos de literatura española*. Besides these essays on erudite matters Reyes wrote books of impressions, *Cartones de Madrid* (1917), of philosophical themes, *El Suicida* (1917) and, of especial importance, *Visión de Anáhuac* (1917), a poetical description of the Mexican plateau.

His collection *Tren de ondas* (1932), written in a lighter vein, has an unsophisticated charm. Here we find the delightful short essay "Diego Rivera Discovers Painting" and the meaningful *Los motivos de la conducta*, an exercise in Semantics which every starchy philologist should read. The definition of "caballero" and "gentleman" is a jewel: to the theory that "caballero" is romantic and "gentleman," classic, Reyes adds his own: "gentleman" is rather dry, "caballero is humid, rather foamy." In this little volume we find the essays on flies, discarded shaving blades, onions ("Dignity of the Onion"), humble topics lifted later to an artistic level by Pablo Neruda in his *Odas elementales* and by Camilo José Cela in his novel *Mrs. Caldwell habla con su hijo*.

Four short essays (*Discursos por Virgilio* (1931), *Atenea política* (1932), *En el día americano* (1932), *Homilía por la cultura* (1938), are, according to Manuel Olguín (*Alfonso Reyes, ensayista*, pp. 74–77), of importance because they contain his first attempts to formulate a social and cultural philosophy. The purpose of these essays is to define the philosophical nature of culture and the duties imposed by it on the intellectual. Reyes wishes to solve the main problems of his social philosophy: to find the formula to raise Spanish America to the level of universal culture, without abandoning the fundamental human values of its Latin and Hispanic tradition.

"Culture," according to Olguín, is defined in these essays as the product of intelligence in its most characteristic function: that of unifying, of establishing regular systems of connections. This function is realized in the horizontal order of "space," or communication among neighbors, and then it is called "cosmopolitism," and in a vertical order of "time," communication among generations, and is called "tradition." Cosmopolitism represents the effort of intelligence to unify man spiritually, to place the principle of fundamental human unity above racial or class iniquities, to distribute equitably the material and spiritual benefits of culture, to make of this planet a more just and happier dwelling place for everybody. Tradition signifies the effort of the intelligence to unify itself, to establish the continuity of its action through time, to consolidate the new generations' enjoyments of its previous conquests. As a servant of intelligence, mother of culture, the intellectual, no matter from what country, has the duty of struggling to impose the cosmopolitan ideal, to improve relations among men. This duty is particularly pressing for the Latin American intellectual, since the progress of Latin America, its ascension to a universal level of culture, depend largely on its union, on its democratization, and on the wise use of the mixture of races and cultures which is now being realized throughout the world.

The natural vehicle to achieve this solution in our continent is that of the fundamental human values of its Latin and Hispanic tradition. These are the values—and not those of the aboriginal cultures—that constitute the real nucleus of its culture. From here it must start, then, to realize its destiny: the creation of a cosmic race, of a closer, happier, fairer New World.

Here, then, we have the expression of the social philosophy of Alfonso Reyes, a philosophy that we find in later books such as *Norte y Sur* (1944) and *Los trabajos y los días* (1945).

Finally, among his strictly literary works of later years, we must mention *Pasado inmediato* (1941), *El deslinde* (1944), *Letras de la Nueva España* (1948), *Grata compañía* (1948), *Trayectoria de Goethe* (1954).

El deslinde, a treatise on literary theory, is considered the masterpiece of Reyes.

Because Alfonso Reyes was a learned man who undertook in America the study of the languages and literatures of Greece and Rome, he may be called a humanist. Reyes knew from early youth that humanism is an endless effort to penetrate the classic cultures, a systematic study and a profound knowledge of those civilizations. Besides, he knew that it also meant a deep knowledge and an intimate love of man. An original aspect of his humanism is his feeling of social responsibility, almost a direct and realistic desire to create an American utopia in which to aspire to the salvation of the individual. The poet who wrote the beautiful pages of *Homero en Cuernavaca* wanted to create a Hellenic society for the man of Mexico.

Like José Enrique Rodó he fought for the universality of knowledge against narrow specialization and was influential in keeping away from our shores the heavy waves of Germanic philology. As early as 1908 he had written his essay on the three Electras of the Athenian theater. He had created a Greece all his own, a land of beauty and serenity where his disturbed soul found solace. The choruses of the Greek tragedy who preach submission to the gods had given him a definitive moral lesson; the inspiration of literature was healing a soul that otherwise might have perished in the vortex of youth and in the asphyxiating atmosphere of a dictatorial political regime. This was for Reyes the first meaning of humanism.

An extensive knowledge of Greek literature is evident in Reyes's basic books, *La crítica en la edad ateniense* (1941) and *La antigua retórica* (1943). His books of essays, *Junta de sombras*, also showed this preoccupation. Of real significance in this field are also *Panorama de la religión griega* (1948), *El horizonte económico en los albores de Grecia* (1950), and *En torno al estudio de la religión griega* (1951).

His main sources of inspiration for the first two works are the theories of Plato (Reyes is baffled by Plato's duality, his belief in the divine origin of poetry, and his disdain for the poet), and the theories of Aristotle. Reyes gives us a detailed biography of Aristotle and a condensation of his philosophy. Reyes was also familiar with the aesthetic ideas of the peripatetic school, especially of that of Theophrastus.

La antigua retórica is described by Reyes himself: "We devoted the second book to rhetoric, centering it on its great organizers —Aristotle, Cicero, and Quintilian—in order to free ourselves of the immense oratorical bulk, passing from Greece to Rome and coming close to the dawn of the Christian era."

El deslinde marks the most ambitious attempt to systematize literary theory: it is a philosophic and aesthetic study of literature.

Reyes tries to establish a demarcation between literature and non-literature, in three sections: 1. Demarcation between pure literature and service literature; 2. A demarcation between history, science, and literature; and 3. A demarcation between mathematics, theology, and literature.

In a very penetrating study of Alfonso Reyes: (*Dos estudios sobre Alfonso Reyes*, Madrid, Insula, 1962) the distinguished Swedish scholar, Ingemar Düring, says that the Mexican author is able to capture in his short stories old images and past experiences, with the vision of a great poet. According to him Reyes shows his capacity as a fiction writer when he sees the heroes of great literature—Achilles, Don Quixote, Hamlet, Peer Gynt—more real than many historical heroes. "Reyes has felt and lived with those heroes the highest form of poetry." Some of these heroes appear in imaginary conversations, in which we find a subtle joke on Landor and his singular conception of Greece. In these pages we perceive Reyes' *lentus risus*, his Horacian virtue of laughing somewhat ironically at himself. Through the light and spiritual dialogue we hear another voice, that of the philosopher and the critic: an intellectual game of the highest level.

There is, then, in this essayist a potential fiction writer. Greek mythology is for him a rich field where his imagination may frolic; the landscape of his native country tempts the descriptive capacity of his talent; the beings or ghosts that he carries in his subconscious are eager to become protagonists of his near-novels. Thus we see them in his *Quince presencias*, and in his poem *Los siete sobre Deva*, which is a prelude to a novel.

His favorite theory is that the landscape can serve as inspiration for the novelist and that in the memory of all human beings there are many elements of fiction. To bring these creatures into the artistic world is the role of the novelist. Therefore, Reyes is a very modern novelist. He does not deal with plots, dramatic developments, or narrations: he creates climates, he analyzes situations very much like a surrealist. It is for this reason that he speaks of his "arranques de novela" ("beginnings of a novel"), novels that are never completed, such as *El testimonio de Juan Peña* (1930).

A good "arranque de novela" is *Los dos augures*. Two Mexican

émigrés meet in Paris and in a brief dialogue they tell of their
past experiences and reveal their inner thoughts. One is a descendant of Spaniards; the other a half-breed. The two friends give
promise of being the two main characters of a novel that never
develops. A pity!—to judge by this beginning characterization:
"Domingo was a courteous Mexican, discreet, patient, gentle, full
of Mexican reserve. If he had not been good, Domingo would
have furnished the best wood from which to carve the statue of
a traitor . . . but he was good." Reyes gives a few more psy-
chological touches to round out his character, and then he stops
short. The reader is disappointed and frustrated. We have the
protagonists, we know their reactions and their experiences, but
nothing happens. The same is true of his *Arbol de pólvora* (1953),
Los siete sobre Deva (1942); but he shows more structural ability
in the surrealist short story *La cena* (1920) and in his short novel
Los tres tesoros (1955).

Reyes is one of the most logical thinkers of his time. His
exposition is clear and well balanced. Since he has said that the
word is the essence of the extension of the poet's world, he is extremely careful in his use of words. His phrase is brief, synthetic,
epigramatic. He uses sometimes an elegant and perfect form, or a
light, graceful expression, according to the subject matter. His
language is rich and alive, strictly literary or robustly vernacular,
classic, without disdain of the use of the Mexican idiom; in short
he is the outstanding cultivator of the artistic style in modern
Mexican literature.

Reyes' death in 1959 was a great loss for Hispanic culture, first
for Mexico, then for Latin America, lastly for Spain. If his creative labors had come to an end several years previously, there still
remained his deep respect for literature, his absolute devotion to
daily work, his perseverance.

His library, original and rich, was a kaleidoscopic world, popu-
lated by poets, philosophers, genii, goblins, enchanters, with
whom Reyes discussed, quarreled, and laughed, every day of
the year; and it was also his workshop where the Master wrote
his poems, his essays, and his books. The giddy life of Mexico
City did not enter his library; the heavy wave of civic turbulence
came to die softly at his door because his ears were deaf to the

political upheaval or to the social struggle. Reyes was in the good company of Homer, Goethe, and Cervantes. His secret retreat protected him from the attacks of gross reality, gave wings to his thoughts, and independence to his ideas. Only in his recess did he feel free from the low nationalism of the day, from the neurotic desire to prove his achievements, from empty declarations and vain postures. He was a Diogenes of Anáhuac! And if somebody had asked him, "Do you want something?" he would have answered: "Yes, that you don't take away my library!"

In the last years of his life Reyes put in order his papers, classified his correspondence, wrote brief notes to his friends, answered all kinds of queries, read one book and wrote one article daily, and prepared new editions of his own works. This superactivity of Alfonso Reyes was an example to his friends; this complete surrender to his professional chores was a moral lesson in a society permeated with materialistic views; this heroic struggle to save his literary work from oblivion, instead of being a selfish one, became a most noble occupation.

Alfonso did not walk in the same path as most Mexican writers of his time; he did not write "novels of the Mexican revolution"; he did not follow the easy formula of the avant-garde poet. When he was reproached for not revealing the pulse of the people in his writings he used to smile, and he was accustomed to judge with severity those young writers who spent their time in the cafés. Of course, age had much to do with this attitude. Young Reyes had spent much time in café life in Madrid, Paris, Rio de Janeiro, and Mexico. In all these countries writers and artists were his closest friends, and he did not refuse the company of beautiful women. Yet, he devoted his best moments to libraries and museums, art galleries, and archives. Diogenes appears only in his old age.

When I knew Alfonso he was already indifferent to his circumstances. His favorite conversation was about classic and old cultures. This was a continuation of his early enthusiasms, of the days of his literary formation when erudition and the knowledge of antiquity were his daily bread. Let us remember that he belonged to a generation of scholars and thinkers, of poets and painters. We must remember this fact in order to understand the last years of his life, his relative isolation, his calculated distance from a group of young writers strongly conscious of their society, from a generation of literary surgeons, and of imitative existentialists, a group of literary patriots who are inventing *"the Mexican"* in the eleventh hour of history.

The typical man of Mexico, like the typical man of Latin America, is the one who can carry well within his blood the culture of the Occidental world. In this regard, Alfonso Reyes was loyal to the voice of his blood and of his heart; he was loyal to Greece, to Rome, to France, to Spain, and to Mexico . . . above all to Mexico.

There is no other Master more noble. Master by example, by doctrine, by vitality, and by love. There is no more civilized man than this, so humble in the understanding and the accomplishing of his high mission.

Let us try to summarize the traits of Alfonso's personality. His most striking and evident characteristic was his gift of courtesy, an inborn quality of the Mexican race, though in him it was not only a physical characteristic, but a revelation of a kind and cordial spirit. It is true that as a person he was graceful, elegant, measured, Attic; that he was refined in conversation and in gestures, but his sense of courtesy was deeper, it emanated from the soul.

His proverbial sense of humor was perhaps a subtle means of softening the sharp edges of reality, a pious way of changing laughter into smile, of criticizing without hurting. Whatever it was to others, it was a great satisfaction to him, a sort of mental gymnastics that lightened the most serious conversations.

Early in life Reyes discovered that artistic success depended on natural talent and hard work, and so all his efforts tended to integrate these two elements. Vocation and dedication were the factors that made possible that extraordinary output of intellectual work, and for this reason he attributed such importance to mental and physical discipline, another classic trait of his personality.

Reyes had a universal conception of art and culture. He knew that Mexico had important values to contribute, but that these values had to be placed on the levels of a cosmopolitan perspective, already dignified with a classic distinction. He also believed in moral and intellectual perfectibility, that art had a moral significance, and that this force should be placed at the service of man. However, under no circumstance could the artist sacrifice its aesthetic principles.

Finally, Alfonso Reyes believed in the sacred mission of the writer, and to this cult he devoted his life. Perhaps this devotion was the strength of his conduct, this certainty that there was nothing superior to creative capacity and intellectual integrity. These ideals oriented his existence and pointed out to him his limitations, and while his friends were wasting energies in the political arena or in the quest for financial power, he was quietly cultivating his garden and preparing his immortality.

Berkeley, 1964   ARTURO TORRES-RIOSECO

Roots: Prologue for a Film

Mexico is at once a world of mystery and clarity: clarity in her landscape, mystery in the souls of her people. The dazzling light sculptures objects and brings them close, naked and glowing, offering temptations to the eyes. Mountains shimmer in the distance; on the volcanoes snow glistens amid rose and silver tints; eagles soar serenely out of sight in the deep blue, "like nails that sink in slowly," says Manuel José Othón, our poet of the deserts. There is no mist, only clouds, bright-edged and so firmly molded they seem almost tangible. Instead of color there are strong contrasts of light and shade; the effect is stark sincerity.

But there is contrast also in the hearts of the people, by turns timid and violent. Despite their long history, and an intensity of suffering equivalent to as many more centuries of earthly travail, they have not yet expended their wellsprings of emotion.

If there can be such a thing as an indefinite age, when one is both young and old, when all time meets in the present, bringing vapors out of the past and a breeze from the future, then this is the age of our people, in whose depths of consciousness, as in a protracted nightmare, the fierce hosts of Cuauhtémoc, last of the Aztec emperors, fight on even now with the iron-clad squadrons of the Spanish conquistador, Cortés. And, all the while, there loom on the horizon the audacious structures of a society still in gestation.

Portentous ruins of Indian cities, which seem to have grown naturally out of the soil; temples and pyramids wrapped in a spiny bristly mantle of cactus, the hostile and heraldic plant entwined by the symbolic serpent, as in the caduceus; solemn and stately colonial buildings, reminiscent of the cuirasses, breastplates, and gauntlets of war; or the fantastic upward-leaping and spiraling Mexican churrigueresque, in which the stone emulates flame; the sweet simplicity of the ranches and little country chapels . . .

The typical Mexico of the countryside is by now familiar to us all, and has a counterpart in the "Spain of the tambourine": the long drawn-out sighing of guitars and songs in falsetto; cockfights; horsemanship and tricks with the lasso; horses in droves; horsemen with silver trappings, wide-brimmed hat, pistol, and machete; men who carry valor to the extreme of temerity; mestizos of sly astuteness; women who hide in shawls, barely revealing the artillery of their sad black eyes. And all this is a part of the truth. But behind this stage setting of striking figures and gaudy colors there are hidden feelings, passions, virtues that cannot be represented by what is merely picturesque.

We have here some Mexican scenes from the stories of Francisco Rojas González, who was prematurely snatched from our affection and admiration when he was yet young in his art. We are not shown the whole spectacle of Mexican life. The author brings us only those aspects of Indian life that are most salient and characteristic, profiles which naturally become blurred as the social ascent is made to the cities, where everything is uniform and everybody looks alike. Moreover, impelled by his burning apostolic zeal, Rojas González has a purpose in inviting us to visit this humanity that writhes in poverty, exploitation, pain, and superstition, a humanity that our writers, our artists, our selfless rural schoolteachers, our men of science are striving, day by day, to redeem. In all latitudes, in all countries, there are twilight zones, as here, where life goes to pieces. To make his scenes sharper, Rojas González strips them down to a clear illustration of an anecdote, or, at times, of a simple epigram.*

1956

---

* For the presentation in Europe of the film *Raíces*, by M. Barbachano, directed by B. Alazraki, Teleproducciones, S.A., México, 1954.

I: Memoirs, Origins

I MEANT to begin these memoirs with my birth; but I do not remember having been born, and, as St. Augustine writes: "I laughed in dreams before I laughed awake." I kept going back farther and farther, from my person to my family, and thence to traditions, and thence to ideas. Plato would say, from the memory to the reminiscence; Goethe, from the prologue in the theater to the prologue in the heavens. And I, in a subdued voice, naturally, put it rather thus: from the definitive land of my birth, in Monterrey, back to the land of my origins, in Guadalajara, the cradle of my forebears, and from there back to the clouds. After all, what the poet calls our residence on earth begins and ends beyond our reach, and we are unraveled on the borderline. I will descend, then, from the clouds, and will touch earth any moment now, first as a dispersed entity, later as a definite person. I suspect, at any rate, that the preludes are worth more than the sonata. I begin, in short, before the beginning.

Some philosophers have fancied that the Creation—the Son— is nothing more than a dialogue between the Father and the Holy Ghost, a *sacra conversazione*, similar to those the artists of old used to paint. The Book of Job and the drama of Faust try to convince us that the history of man is a wager between the Lord and the Rebel Angel.

For a creature so humble as the one we are going to talk about, there is no need to go back very far. Far enough, and near enough, are the titans who have been godfathers to the human race: the foolish Epimetheus, who was passing foolish, and his brother the clever Prometheus, who was passing clever, as we all remember. One gave us the weight of the past; the other the alleviation of the future. And thus there became intermingled the qualities that each of us bears witness to: vices and virtues, capacities for joy and sorrow, and even our paired dimensions in time and space—above and below, yesterday and tomorrow—in order to compound this bipolar nature that afflicts us today, and that all the primitive fables try to justify, or at least to explain in some manner.

In my own case, the homunculus fell into the hands of an irresponsible demiurge who, on top of the basic metaphysical conflicts, still took pleasure in confounding castes and tribes, and the bloods and humors that go along with them. Oh, God, oh gods! How could such an intermixture of atavisms take place? As if it were not enough that this pagan enamored of the Mediterranean should suddenly feel like an Asiatic, there were added to him condiments of Reyes from Andalusia and La Mancha, of Ochoas from Navarre, the extremes and the center of Iberia; tossed together in the crucible were the Hispanic substance and the American Indian, so that, there within, during the black hours of insomnia, Cortés and Cuauhtémoc go on fighting battles (for, as the saying goes, "in Mexico, what we have of Cortés does not do away with Cuauhtémoc"); a dash of seasoning from France and the Netherlands was mixed in, and, finally, the rude loaves of Gerona, for from there I get the name Ogazón.

In the present, the solar and Apollonian influences of the man who engendered me, blond and blue-eyed, meet with interference on contact with the somewhat melancholy lunar rays of the dark woman who conceived me. But, besides, each gust contributes its bit from some other region beyond the horizon. Afterward, culture took charge of the results: I had either to take the entire world for my own, or find myself disinherited. There was no other choice.

> The rooster Chantecler said to the dog Patou:
> "It seems to me, you are of a strange race.
> What are you, after all?" "I am a weird mixture,
> A combination dog that barks with every howl ever heard.

All the different bloods beat together within me:
Griffin, mastiff, pointer from the Artois or Sansueña,
A whole pack of hounds sleeps within my soul.
Oh rooster! I am really all dogs put together."
   (And Chantecler, protective and optimist:)
"That explains the sum of your immense goodness."

What a catastrophe the history of my soul would have been, if I had not learned to accept these mixtures within me as a thing to be taken for granted. But I soon became convinced that they are basic in all authentic cultures, in those that create, at least, if not in those that merely imitate. What a constant anguish my work would have been if I had not learned in time that the only true punishment is in the confusion of tongues, and not in the confusion of bloods! Let me explain:

The art of expression, it seemed to me, was no mere rhetorical exercise, divorced from conduct, but rather the richest means of expressing human feeling. The harmony we yearn for, the talisman that reduces the contradictory impulses of our nature to order, could be found, I believed, in the word. Certain personalities, it has occurred to me to say somewhere, can achieve coherence only in the point of a pen. The practice of writing became for me a transcendental force that pervaded and guided my whole being. For stones, plants, and animals, to exist may mean something else. For a man—so far as he is a man—to exist fully is to transform that other thing, that basic sustenance, into feeling and thought, and the "catharsis" for this is the word. Apart from the privileged moments of mystic ecstasy—which do not often come within the mandate of our will—this metamorphosis finds its proper and accessible instrument in the disciplines of speech. The word is the final earthly epitome of human conclusions, and the rest of the voyage belongs to the realm of religion. After all, it is not Patou alone who must fight his way through armies of horrid monsters. We were put into the world to meet this trial and to perform this duty. The biological background is always more or less heterogeneous and confused. To classify it, there comes the Logos, a term which, for the Greeks, summed up both speech and spirit, and which the Christian took over with only a change of emphasis, carrying it to the final and sublime phase. . . .

And it was my good fortune that, for the attainment of so

transcendental an end—the Logos in the Savior—I had been provided with a means so simple and down-to-earth and within the scope of mouth and hand as the business of uttering words with the breath or threading them together with the pen. Do I make it clear what the practice of letters has meant to me? Double redemption by the word: first through the concord of bloods; second through the shaping of the personality, in its relation to others as well as in its own inner growth.

And if some day the bridge of death must be commemorated by an evocative line, let them write on my tomb: HERE LIES A MINOR SON OF THE WORD.

II: ONE OF THE PEOPLE

The truth is, I have no clear idea of my family background. What little I do know has come to me in gusts and snatches, and I never inspected the genealogical trees and minute records which, I am told, some of my Guadalajara kin have painstakingly compiled.

When my father was Secretary of War and of the Navy and regarded as the likely heir to the throne of Porfirio Díaz, a King of Arms made his appearance, a heraldist, bringing a purported history of our lineage that commenced, of course, with the Crusades. Prominent among our forebears was St. Bernard himself, founder of Clairvaux, opponent of Abelard and of Arnaldo of Brescia, preacher of the Second Crusade, fortunate supporter of Innocent II in the schism with Anacletus, author of celebrated letters and treatises, monk in armor, and patron saint of my father, who, although refusing to acknowledge him as such, nevertheless also celebrated his own birthday on the twentieth of August.

The coat of arms, as I recall it, was not in bad taste, though I would never be able to reconstruct it. The album was buried in my father's library, where I—then going on eleven years—was in the habit of squandering long hours. I came upon it and set out to peruse it. I strongly suspected that all these grandeurs were worth no more than bread and pickles in a painting. But I amused myself by taking them for a base on which to fabricate lovely fictions. Like the ancient Greeks, I could be satisfied, in the absence of a definite prehistory, with a mythology.

I was not allowed to keep my toy. My elder brothers, in my

father's presence, made me the butt of a joke that had dire consequences. "Did you know," they said to him, "this boy is going to have the Crusaders' coat of arms embroidered on his Sunday shirts?"

This, even as a joke, was too much for that liberal prince, whose grandeur had no use for ancient quarterings. Quarters, he understood, were something to be furnished to his troops in the wars of the Republic; quarter was something you did not give to the enemy. He was leery of the contagion that this subtle fraud might spread: how often vain notions begin in games, then one day they topple the wavering reason. He decided to play safe, to cut the nonsense short, and had all my fictitious nobility consigned to the flames.

Perhaps it was just as well. I am a man of the people, and like every son of the Americas, in default of patrician lineage I am heir to the whole world. No blue blood, nor even local color of too deep a dye. My family was a family on horseback. Our home itself shifted about, on the trail of my father's campaign, and the provincial hearth was always somewhat blurred by distance. My roots are rooted in change. I was destined to be a traveler. My home is the earth. I have never felt profoundly a stranger amongst any people, even though I have always been in the position of one shipwrecked on this planet, despite the artificial fence that my diplomatic duties seemed to require me to take along everywhere. I am brother to many men and speak intimately with people of many lands. Wherever I go I am drawn by ties of truth.

The deep root, unconscious and involuntary, is in my American being, which is a fact and not a virtue. It has been the cause of rejoicing, but also of bloody tears. I do not need to invoke it on every page in order to please fools, nor do I intend to discount the rewards of my modest labor with patriotic fraud. Without any effort or merit on my part, it manifests itself in all my books and imbues all my thoughts like the exhalation of growing plants. It takes care of itself. As for my own choice, I do not want to be weighed down by any shackles of tradition. The universal heritage is mine by right of love, and by work and study, and these are the only titles that hold good.

Thoughts on
the Ninth of February

SEVENTEEN YEARS ago my poor father died. It is not his presence in the flesh that I most sorely miss: since I had to live, as a student, in Mexico City, far from Monterrey, I grew accustomed to seeing him but rarely and to conjuring him up at will, a feat made easy for me by his positive, clear-cut personality and even his physical aspect, so cleanly drawn and finely chiseled— his peculiar kind of beauty. Since he was such a busy man, I expected little else from him, beyond an occasional letter of almost formal greeting, couched in his secretary's style. And, incidentally, that reminds me of the letter that his childhood friend Doña Lola Mora—Mrs. Lancaster Jones—once wrote to him in reproach for those impersonal answers his secretary Zuñiga used to redact; it began with this salutation: "My Dear Zuñiga, I have received yours bearing date of . . ."

For several years I saw my father only during vacations and short visits. Those few days, to be sure, more than made up for the long absences, because his was one of those natures that penetrate and pervade and imbue everything around them. When I was near him I wanted nothing but to remain by his side. When I was far away, the very thought of him would bring me the warmth of his presence. His mind, ceaselessy active, was continually giving forth the most delightful and provocative notions; and all his ideas were fresh, glowing, newly forged by a sensibility like none other I have encountered in my wide experience of men. In truth, even my literary curiosity found reward in my father's company. He lived in the provincial city of Monterrey. I live in Mexico, the capital. He was more than forty years older than I, and had been formed by the belated romantic movement in our America. He was a soldier and a statesman. I aimed to be a writer. None of these things made any difference. While my elder brothers in the capital, university men with an intellectual background, were looking askance at the new trends in poetry, I, on vacation in Monterrey, found my father reading with enthusiasm Rubén Darío's *Songs of Life and Hope*, which had just come out.

Nevertheless, I had grown used to my father's absence, and had even learned to riffle through him at a distance, in much the way that we mentally leaf through the pages of a book we know from memory. It was enough for me to be assured that somewhere on earth the heart was beating in which my faintness of spirit—my melancholy, rather—took strength and was comforted. Always it has been an alleviation to recall him. In the hours of deepest despair, when I was most battered and torn by the first passions that racked me, my instinct turned from time to time to remembrance of my father, and that remembrance had the power to revive me and console me. Later, after my father died, I became aware of that unconscious replenishment of my spirit. In his lifetime, I doubt if I ever noticed. . . .

But now it comes to me, I did, indeed, notice, after a fashion. One time when I arrived at Monterrey to spend my vacation it was night. I went to bed and to sleep. In the morning I awoke with a vague feeling of sadness—something that happened to me often in adolescence—as if it would cost me an effort to begin another day of life. Then the automatic mechanism started in to restore my equilibrium. Before my reason could take control, my imagination was talking: "Cheer up," it said to me, "Remember that, after all, yonder in Monterrey, something solid and tangible is waiting for you: your home, your family, your father." Almost at once I realized I was even then on home ground, among my own people and under my father's roof. And the thought that I had exhausted every recourse, that I had already exercised my right of appeal to the highest and final court, so dismayed me and (paradoxically) chilled me with such a sense of abandonment, it was hard for me to hold back my tears. This emotional upset taught me to appreciate the advantages of not drawing too freely on my golden store, and of having my father at a distance, as a last resort, like that vigilant weapon hung by the ranchman on his bedstead, even though he would prefer never to use it. Perhaps I go a little astray in this analysis. It is not easy to explore the volcanic zone of our reticences and our venerations.

Suddenly there came the tremendous shock of my father's death, all the greater because this was an accident, a collision with a physical obstacle, a violent rending of life by a burst of shrapnel, instead of the foreseen and gradually acceptable close that comes from the wearing out of the body. This gave his death the air of an unspeakable cosmogonic jest, of a gross affront to the intentions of creation. My natural sorrow was made more painful by the singularly pathetic and bloody circumstances which surrounded that death and affected not just one family but an entire people. His death came as the climax to a scene of horror that involved the whole city. With my father gone, it seemed to many of his friends and foes alike, that one of the few strong wills capable of mastering destiny had gone. It was as if the fatherland that was doomed to bleed for years to come had begun to bleed with the wounds in his body. Afterward, I tried to mend myself the best way I could, as the poor dogs that lose a paw, crushed by a vehicle in the street, mend themselves and are able to walk and run again; as the one-armed learn to eat with a single hand; as monks learn to live without the world, or invalids without salt. And then I contrived to draw strength from my mutilation. My practiced imagination came to my aid. I pretended my father was absent—a situation long familiar—and set in to leaf him through, as was my custom. Better still, I read him more clearly and with keener insight than before. I succeeded in bringing him close to me, like a sort of atmosphere, like an aura. I taught myself to question him and to receive his answers. To consult him about everything. Little by little I timidly persuaded him to accept criticism which has never passed my lips (but which some of my friends, knowing me well, have divined). Certain differences of opinion between my father and me, which we never put into words, but sensed, like a tender anxiety, were brought out into the open where we could approach agreement. This process went on for several years, during my travels and in foreign climes. At last we arrived at a mutual understanding that I find sufficient. I would not dare hope for a perfect understanding, because I am sure the joy of it would kill me, and intuition tells me I can know communion that is absolute only at the hour of my death. But the process has matured to such a degree that a little more than two years ago, when I was in Paris, I had the temerity to write a friend these words, more or less: "Savages used to believe they acquired the virtues of the enemies they killed. I have better reason to believe we acquire the virtues of the dead if we truly learn to love them." I feel that, from the day of his departure, my father has sought to enter my soul and to make himself at home there. I think I have now absorbed him completely, and I would say, if the word were not so odious— digested him completely. And here we see how, without following religion's ready-made road, my personal experience leads me to the idea of the soul's survival, and even to the idea of the intervention of souls, the only bridge the dead and the living can cross over, paying no customs duty except the adoption of that spiritual attitude which, for brevity's sake, we call prayer.

Since he lived always amidst dangers, and I have always been able to adapt myself (perhaps a natural plasticity had something to do with this), I learned, while yet a small child, to face the prospect of losing him. But the smashing brutal reality of having lost him was such a hard blow, I can assure you I still feel it; not merely because the after effects of that immense wound persist: I still feel the blow itself, in all its shattering force, in some recess of my soul, and know I could recall it totally at will. The happening travels through time, seems to fade in the distance and become a thing of the past, but there is a corner of the mind where it stays on. In the same way, if a person on a certain star should contemplate our world through a powerful telescope, he would see at this moment—for the deed is still alive, whirling like a phantasm of light through sidereal space—Hernán Cortés and his men, spellbound, gazing for the first time at the Valley of Anáhuac.

My hurt was so deep, I, who was by then myself a father, learned a lesson from my suffering. I have made an effort to restrain my natural demonstrations of tenderness, in order not to rear my son amid too many caresses, so he would not miss my physical presence too much when I had to leave him. Hard and authoritarian I could never be—nothing is more repugnant to me than that. But I have tried to be reserved and a bit stolid —only I know with what an effort—and thus have brought up, I believe, a man who is better balanced, better fitted than I was to withstand uprooting. As I battled with the terrible anguish that overwhelmed me at my father's death, I made a firm decision: that I would rather not be too indispensable to my son, or even too much loved by him, since he is bound to lose me. That I should need him is another, quite irremediable matter. My conscience has leaned on him a thousand times, in moments of vacillation. But it is better for him not to need me—I said to myself—though it means I must forego the pleasure of heaping him with endearments. Moreover, I chose to shut my eyes before my father's prostrate form, in order to keep my best image of him intact. Furthermore, I chose to pursue my own free course, casting every impulse to rancor or revenge, no matter how justified, from my heart, rather than to become the slave to a base vendetta. I avoided all who claimed to be eyewitnesses; I imposed silence on those who wanted to tell me the name of the man who opened fire. I know, by taking this course, I have deliberately cut off a part of myself: I know I have lost forever the springs of aggression and ambition. But I have done like the man bitten by a rattlesnake, who chopped off his finger with a stroke of the machete. Anyone who has suffered pain of this kind will understand me.

No, it is not his presence in the flesh that I most sorely miss, warm and magnetic though it was, and with me gentle and tender, inspiring my imagination and enriching my perceptions, showing my esthetic sense how satisfactory a human style can be, gratifying my filial pride, helping me in my sincere apprenticeship to become a man and to become a Mexican (and I have known so few men, and among these so few Mexicans!). I do not weep for the loss of his earthly companionship, since I have acquired a substitute, through sorcery, or, if you prefer, through a miracle. I weep for the injustice that is the self-annihilation of a noble life; I am dismayed, when I consider my father's story, by the feeling that there is something amiss in the obscure moral clockwork of our world; I am moved to despair, when I face the accomplished fact, which is nothing but a tomb, by the thought that here is the whole result of a full and generous existence: not enough to fill the emptiness of a single second. My tears are for the tower of manhood that has come down; for the splendid architecture—the finished product of fine materials brought together and elaborated through centuries of scrupulous inheritance—that just one toss of chance could undo; for the wine of seven consuls whose sugars and spirits were concentrated a long age, and which was casually overturned by a reckless hand.

Now that the wine has been overturned, let it be a sacrifice; this I accept: let it be a beneficent libation for the land that received it.

II

Of all his wounds, the only one apparent was to his right hand, which remained somewhat awkward always and ached in the wintertime. The left hand had to learn from it to write and eat and also to fire arms. But it slowly regained the ability to write. A man who, after fifty, was capable of methodically setting himself to learn a new foreign language was not to be deterred by a trifle.

Browsing in his library, I have come upon the four stages of his signature. The first, elegant, full-blown, curvaceous, appears in a volume of Espronceda's poetical works published at Paris in 1867. The second I find in a copy of Heredia's poems, and it is dated, "Mazatlán, 1876." Here his baptismal name is reduced to the initial and the script is lighter and more nervous, while the same adolescent rubric is retained with all its involuted hearts and flourishes. The third phase I find in private letters to the poet Manuel José Othón, around 1889. Though subsequent to the wound, it is still rather ornate. The fourth phase is the well-known one that the documents of his governorship exhibit: the spare, terse, mechanical signature of the official.

III

But we have come into his library; this means the horse is unsaddled. In that library, which contained something of everything, books of poetry and literary classics abounded. Among the poets, the romantics prevailed: it was their intellectual heyday when the hero's mind was being formed. The discovery of that juvenile signature in a copy of Espronceda's poems has a special significance.

After he had pacified the North and put a stop to contraband on the frontier—where insolent chieftains spawned by the civil wars vied with the grafters who are always among us in lining their pockets with illicit lucre—there came his peaceful years as governor. And because the General, between times, had no work to do for several months, except the monotonous barracks routine, he made use of his leisure to unite in one volume the innumerable tomes of Cesar Cantu's *History of Mankind* (Historia de la Humanidad). Only the titanic enterprise could attract and hold his interest. Even if it turned out to be methodically titanic, like his government of Nuevo Leon. Others can tell what he accomplished in that state and in the city of Monterrey. Here the romantic relaxed, or, to put it more accurately, restrained his energies and harnessed the thunderbolt with administration— the watchword of the Porfirian Peace. The cascade was diverted into gracious rivulets, and these, little by little, transformed the desert into a fertile garden. The hero's popularity soared. Jealous messengers began to arrive from the capital. Finally, Porfirio Díaz himself came to witness the miracle. "That's the way to govern," was his verdict. And before long the Governor was taking charge of the Ministry of War, where he had occasion to bring about other miracles: installing a voluntary military service, weaning the people from their Sunday vices by inducing them to flock with spontaneous enthusiasm to the drilling fields; building a collective self-discipline that should be the natural way of a democracy; educating the army to accept the loftiest social ideals of that time; propagating confidence in the country when skepticism was in fashion; opening the doors to hope for a better day. A new spirit was being molded in the warmth of his love. This everyone knows who was on the scene; those who deny it know they deceive. That love, spread over a whole people, was like a rich carpet of red carnations covering a field.

Another man would have taken advantage of his opportunity. But he was not one for schemes, this great romantic! They offered him a ready-made, almost bloodless revolution—and he rejected it! Below, armies and cities were waiting, and the entire country hoping for the chance to obey him, watching for the slightest sign of wavering in the hero. Above, in Galeana, in the austere air of the mountain peaks, was a man alone. And, to bring him out of that ecstasy, the river had to surge from its bed and carry away half the city of Monterrey. Then he asked for his horse again and went over the rugged path to help the citizens. A little later, he was off to a foreign land. There was no room in the circle for two centers. Or, there had to happen what happens in the living cell when the nuclei begin to form. Put the country in the plight of having to retrace its history? It was better to weigh anchor.

The land's blurred outline is no longer in sight. It is all gone.

IV

Porfirio Díaz turned the situation over to the new authorities and made one of his characteristic remarks:

"Well, they've let the mares loose! Let's see who can corral them again!"

Hell is paved with good intentions. And when, in spite of the best intentions that have ever been shown in Mexico, the country insisted on coming to pieces, how could the great romantic avoid being regarded as the man of destiny? During some maneuvers that he watched in France, he felt a burning in his left eye, he put a patch on it and continued to follow the movements of the troops. On his return from the field—and to his death he concealed this from everyone—he found he had lost half his sight. Thus he returned to the country, when his natural decline had commenced. Still unsettled by that intoxicating popularity, and by the superhuman effort he had made to throw it off, his perception of reality distorted now by the abrupt change in our atmosphere, which, to the elder generation, amounted to the amputation of good sense, he came, although reluctantly, to represent the last hope of those who were out of step with life. Alas, second parts have never been good! Now he was not wanted: he was left alone. He followed a despairing road from one disappointment to another. Something inside him had broken. He did not want to hang up his shield in the arsenal. How much better if he had done so! Whenever has the emeritus returned to mingle again with the legions? The years and the hurts had done their work.

He found himself involved in a web of mischance that grew ever denser and blacker. A thousand obstacles and his great friends on both sides prevented an agreement between the future president, Francisco Madero, and himself. Again he left the country. And finally we see him symbolically crossing back over the Rio Grande, accompanied by half a dozen friends and making his way to the northern haciendas where he had been promised men and aid and where he found only betrayal.

The days passed, and the promises were not fulfilled. As the scanty file neared the Conchos River, a few rural guards began to snipe at it. All scattered, in one direction or another, and left him alone with his guide.

It was Christmas Eve. The landscape was cold and desolate. The first thing to do was spur on and find a safe spot to meditate in for a while. And through briars and thorns that tore his clothes and covered his body with scratches, the guide led him to a solitary spot. It was a good place for meditation in a melancholy vein. There was not a growing thing to be seen, save those inhospitable thickets. The horseman dismounted, gathered his thoughts, and once again the flame of sacrifice was lighted in his heart.

"Where is the nearest military post?"

"At Linares."

"Let's go to Linares."

"They'll kill us."

"When we're in sight of the city you can make your getaway and leave me on my own."

Now it is night, Christmas night. The muffled figure approaches the corporal of the guard.

"I wish to speak to the officer."

In a moment the officer comes to the door. The muffled face is uncovered. And the officer almost falls to his knees.

"Go away, quickly, my General! Don't you know it's my duty to arrest you?"

"So it's you, my good friend, my old groom? Well, there's nothing for you to do but turn your troops over to me, or else take me prisoner."

"Sir, there are very few of us!"

"Then I am going to raise my voice so they can all hear me:
I have come to deliver myself up, and you may shoot me here on
the post."

The townspeople have found clothes for him; his were in
shreds. They make no attempt to dissemble their pity, their
respect. They sense that a whole era of human feeling has surrendered with this man. Once again he offers up his life. What
better thing could the romantic do with his life? Throw it over-
board, drop it out the window! "A tiny hair tossed into the
sea!" says the romantic. And he tosses his heart to the waves.

V

Later, in Mexico City, he wore himself out in prison, where the
pathetic uncertainties of the times kept him secluded month after
month. The pine table, the depressing kerosene lamp, the hand
cupping the forehead, the confusion of meditation and memory,
and all the clangor of "Diablo Mundo"—this is, line for line, the
picture in Espronceda's poem. That poet so dear to him, whose
verses he himself taught me to recite!

In the courtyard the prisoners sing; they stretch out in the
sun, deal cards. This is like a running sore on the military or-
ganism. One day each week the camp followers are allowed in
the courtyard, where they set up canvas tents to hide their
travesty of love. After the owner is satisfied, he stands in front
of the tent and charges the others a few centavos for admission.
The sight of these things was a truly diabolical torture for the
man who, like none other, had been the organizer of model
armies, who had raised the military class, in the nation's eyes, to
a new dignity.

Melancholy and failing health brought back the malaria he had
contracted on campaign. Every evening at the same hour the
phantasm of fever called at his door. His nerves were wearing
thin. He lived as in an intermittent nightmare. Which was
delirium? Which was reality? The prisoner was treated with
extraordinary consideration, and the good man who was president, although he felt compelled to imprison him, would have
liked nothing better than to let him go free. Two great souls
confronted each other, attracted, perhaps, through vast distances
of starry space. One all dash and fire, and the other all simplicity

and candor. Each completed his tragic course, and who knows with what secret reluctance they took their different ways. Some day there will be revelations. Some day we will learn of overtures that perhaps came too late.

Under certain conditions, then, the prisoner could receive visitors. Among the friends who approached him in his misfortune there were naturally many who, bound by old affections, come to us like breezes out of the past, laden with memories of childhood and happy days. Such visits, however comforting they might seem to be, deeply exacerbate the sensibilities of a man who is overwrought, and in between attacks of fever, when a clear view of that foul prison returned to his consciousness like a bad taste, here would come those men and those women, overflowing with recollections, full of words saturated with feeling, too emotional to be good for a man who was going through a crisis. Everything should have been neutral, gray. And everything was clamorous and scarlet.

And as if anything further were needed to drive him mad, on top of the tragic widowing of one daughter, whose husband had been murdered a few months earlier, there came the news of the brigandage committed by the chieftain Urbina, the one who died by being swallowed up in mire. Urbina had kidnapped his youngest daughter's husband, and she had been forced to ransom him at a terrible price, jeopardizing for a lifetime the economic security of her home. Imagine the Paladin's fury at the outrages suffered by his daughters.

He was not an old man yet; he had not yet given up, but he began to find it difficult to grope his way through the spiderwebs of fever, melancholy, exasperation, and remembrance.

Pancho Villa also was confined during those months, in the military prison of Santiago. Soon Pancho Villa would make his escape, with the connivance of his guards, and thanks to the efforts of the lawyer Bonales Sandoval, who was later knifed, carved into pieces, stuffed in a sack, and sent, loaded on a mule, to Félix Díaz, by Villa's orders, as punishment for having tried to create an understanding between the two generals. It may be that the knight and the guerrilla chieftain crossed paths in the prison corridors. It would have been like Don Quixote and Roque Guinart contemplating each other. The chieftain would size him up from afar, with that peculiar smile of his and that dropped eyelid. The knight would stroke his beard in the manner of his youth and recall his campaigns against the Tiger of Alica, that other born strategist produced by our soil, who similarly mixed evil deeds with great achievements.

The vision fades and another appears: now it is of cheering multitudes, exalted by burning words that fall from the height of a balcony, rolling like globes of fire; that multanimous being shudders with emotion and offers thousands of hands and thousands of hearts. But this vision is inebriating, deceptive, and soon disappears—a temptation caught up in a kerchief and cast away—and other memories take its place.

VI

That daily gnawing on his nerves was leaving them raw, exposing his sensibility. One day he asked me to recite some Christmas verses. This was his last Christmas and the anniversary of the sad night at Linares. When I got to the words: "You have been made evil by sorrow's blows," he covered my mouth with his hands and shouted to me:

"Silence, blasphemer! False, every word! Those who have not lived the words cannot know the meaning of them!"

Then I understood that he had lived the words, that he had composed poetry with his life, that he himself was a poem in motion, a romantic poem, of which he was the author and, at the same time, the protagonist. I have never known a case of more perfect interfusion between poetry and life. He thought of himself, naturally, as a man of action, for to give oneself to dreaming seemed to him an abominable form of egoism. But he saw no difference between imagination and action, he was so plastic to the dream. There is no explanation, otherwise, for his having hurled his copy of Quevedo from him one day—respectful as he was of the classics—exclaiming with his fine vehemence: "He lies! He lies!" He had come upon the following passage:

"Whoever it was called letters and arms sister arts knew little about either one, for no two things can be more different than doing and saying." He lies! He lies! And the poet on horseback goes about amongst humanity performing actions that are nothing but dreams. As dreams or as actions they were without self-interest: actions offered to others for the benefit of others, and in the performance of them the fuel of his overflowing vitality was spent.

Where have we seen before this tuft of blond beard, the blue eyes, the imposing brow? The heavy eyebrows of an old hidalgo, the gaze of a confident eaglet taking the measure of its prey in the air, the smile of a spotless conscience and the ringing laughter of a man without fear. The strong boot with the tiny bell on its single-pointed spur, the sabre clanking on its chain. The air of Apollo sometimes, and sometimes the air of Jupiter, depending on whether the expression is bland with serene peace or all knotted between the formidable brows. There, between the eyes, are poetry and action in explosive bursts. From there a will that has the substance of a song shoots its arrows. We have seen all this before, surely, in the Ideal: the Ideal of the Hero, of the Warrior, of the Romantic, of the Knight Errant, of the Poet of Chivalry. Because he was, in his whole appearance and in his manners, the perfect embodiment of chivalry.

Again the cannon roared. The guards, their soldierly instinct awakened, themselves broke open the prison gates. What will the Romantic do? What can he do—Oh, heavens!—no matter what happens, no matter who falls (and what true Mexican can fail to understand this?), but leap once more on his horse and take his place in the adventure, at the head of the column, the only place for the Poet. Here I died and was born again, and if anyone wants to know who I am, let him inquire of the shades of February. Whatsoever comes of me, good or bad, can be laid to that bitter day.

When the machine gun had vomited its shrapnel, in a heap of men and horses in the middle of the plaza and in front of the entrance to the National Palace, on a Sunday morning, Mexico's greatest romantic lay dead.

A broad, generous smile was still alive on his face: the last sprig untrodden by Attila's horse; the solitary wisp of grain— oh, Heine!—that the reaper forgot.

Buenos Aires, February 9, 1930.
On August 20, 1930, he would have had his eightieth birthday.

Intimations of America

T HE THEMES joined here in continuous text were written for the most diverse occasions; tucked away in obscure periodicals or limited editions, they had long since commenced their journey to oblivion, or else had begun, as the old saying goes, to "serve as points for alien pens." It seemed high time to collect them; besides, when I read them consecutively I came to new conclusions.

I have often invoked America, focus of all our anxieties, and now the meaning of America was the strongest reality I could grasp. I laid hold on this passage and that, piecing them together in a sort of patchwork; but successive re-touchings brought out a single prevailing thought, and this was strengthened by later revisions and reflections.

The best way to approach America, no doubt, is through contemplation of man's stumbling but inspired progress toward knowledge of the planet's whole configuration. The shadowy magnet hovered over the human mind, making itself felt through mysterious channels. What could be more dramatic than myth resolving into history? * The meaning of such a process on the

---

* The history of the myths that preceded and accompanied the Discovery has been the subject of numerous books, including, in English, Stefan Zweig, *Amerigo, A Comedy of Errors in History* (New York, 1942), and the extremely important work of Samuel Eliot Morison, *Admiral of the Ocean Sea* (New York, 1942, 2 volumes).

geographical plane is simply a reflection of its meaning on the spiritual plane and as a function of the soul.

These pages suffer from incompleteness, in the light of subsequent research, and even fail to make use of all the facts accessible at the time. But I see no point in expanding them in order to transform into a learned treatise what was intended to be nothing more than a suggestion as to the interpretation of certain facts. Nor do I see any point in adding new data if, as I trust, I have succeeded in upholding my thesis. Moreover, he who insists on the last word runs the risk of remaining forever silent in a conversation that never comes to an end. And, as Quintilian warns us, we must some time make up our mind to call our work finished.

In Heaven, On Earth,
Everywhere

E VER SINCE man began to leave a record of his dreams, the likelihood of a new world has appeared in the form of a presage. It was forecast by fantasy some three thousand years before Christ, when somewhere in the mysterious West the mythical Anubis presided over the dead. The notion of an undiscovered region in the West, which at times was a happy kingdom and at times a gloomy sea, dates from the earliest Egyptian documents; its anthropological roots grow deep in a mystic twilight. At times this region was concealed beneath the shimmering ocean. At times it was projected as far as the sun itself.

While the Phoenicians were exploring the western Mediterranean, island by island, and even bringing tin and amber from the secret Atlantic—and, later on, while the Atlantic islands were being conquered by European sailors—the mystery kept receding like the shadow of a traveling cloud; it retreated to the hazy horizon of the sea. This is the meaning of the "Plus Ultra" beyond the Pillars of Hercules. This vagrant notion flutters through the oldest poetry, now as promise, now as threat, crosses the dunes of classical literature, flowers in Plato's portentous Atlantis, thrills the imagination of the Stoics. It travels through Latin letters:

Seneca, in his *Medea,* declares the seas will open wide to reveal unsuspected continents. And, carrying its moving and changing burden, its Sea of Sargasso, its shallow and unnavigable ocean, its Fortunate Islands, it is enriched throughout the Middle Ages with Utopian legends: the Isle of St. Brandan or of the Birds—that earliest version of Penguin Island—the Isle of the Seven Cities, the Antilles or "Islands in Front," and Brazil—names that geography will finally adopt. It takes a boat ride with the poets of the Renaissance. And at last it deposits its cullings of truth and fable in the hands of Christopher Columbus, when he opens the pages of *Imago Mundi,* about the year 1482. This work, by Cardinal Pierre d'Ailly was, indeed, the Discoverer's breviary, and his feverish notes are scribbled on its margins. It is a crazy quilt of all the conjectures that could be assembled about all the paradises that man's yearning had ever devised.

The scattered features of some dismembered truth were trying to join themselves within the soul. The Earth whispered to its creatures hints of its perfect shape, the Platonic entity remembered as in a dream. And thus, America, before she became the solid reality that sometimes exalts and sometimes dismays us, was the invention of poets, the charade of geographers, the gossip of adventurers, the cupidity of traders, and, in sum, a strange craving and a longing to burst bonds. The hour arrives when the presage is read on every forehead, shines in sailors' eyes, robs the humanists of their sleep, and endows commerce with the dignity of science and the exhilaration of high adventure.

As the presage is felt on earth, so is it reflected in heaven. Remember those guesses at stars never seen, whose glimmering is intimated in Aristotle, which declare themselves to Lucan, which glow in the cavern of Dantesque nights, where the constellation of the Four Cardinal Virtues is the fore-image of the Southern Cross; and which still, since the Discovery, shine forth profusely in every form of poetry.

THE AXES OF THE DISCOVERY

Little by little the features of the Earth were filled out.

European history was born in the Mediterranean basin, and particularly in that eastern corner where Greek courage suffered, then fought, then finally routed the ambitions of the sacred oriental empires. Outside the familiar circle, beyond what the eye could see, terror and myth held boundless sway. It was believed that in the north men were made out of snow; in the south, out of charcoal. The solid earth, beyond any doubt, was an island surrounded by water. The belt of the hydrosphere embraced the lithosphere. Above, was the transparent cape of the atmosphere, which had underneath a symmetrical balance in Tartarus. There were some travelers reckless enough to shatter this closed orb. Military ambition and the philosophic dream of "homonoia" expanded the world as far as India, with Alexander's irresistible thrust. But the center still did not move from the sea that was the Greek's true fatherland. The duel between the eastern and the western Mediterranean, between the classical world and Carthage, was not to be won from Syracuse. Rome inherited the duel. Then the Roman conquests ascended to the north, and then the invasions from the north descended on Rome. Europe had reached upward, but still grappled the Mediterranean. Slowly its axes lengthened out to the Atlantic; when the discovery of America succeeded in closing, so to speak, the circle of the Ocean, they became firmly fixed on the western side. Explorers, going inland, were able to furnish precise data for the map makers, who had been content, until then, with drawing monsters and dragons.

Beginning in the twelfth century, when the Basques came ashore on the banks of Newfoundland, and on through the tentative scouting by Bretons and Normans, and into the fifteenth century, when Renaissance culture put vague oral traditions into written form, there was one discovery after another, and in the last decade of the fifteenth century they came thick and fast. The face of the earth was filled out, feature by feature. The west coast of Africa surrendered to sailors and let itself be deciphered little by little. The most astonishing tales were carried from the Orient. Soon these scattered rumors, mere curiosities at first, were resolved into a symphony of excitement. The route to the Indies became a preoccupation, from the day that Constantinople fell to the Turks. Commodities from the East were thus cut off, by the same stroke that released a flow of Byzantine philology into Europe. Centuries earlier, the fall of Miletus to the Persians brought the Ionic philosophers to Italy and Athens. As Athens owed her flowering to the ruin of Miletus, so Italy owed to a similar catastrophe her spiritual dominance in the dawn of modern times. While half of humanity was getting drunk on the wonders of the Renaissance, the other half—the world of traders and adventurers—was going mad with action, with desire for the aromatic islands of spice.

Voyages were the great public and private enterprise of the fifteenth century. Ideas about geography floated in the air like particles of dust. Each pilot was a discoverer. For some of these, to sight land was to discover it; no wonder posterity tends to discount their ambitious claims to title. For others, to discover was to colonize, or at least to organize peaceful trade, or else to capture slaves by force of arms. We see with relative frequency lands discovered two or three times, and also regions, hit upon by chance or by shipwreck, that could never again be identified.

Portugal and Spain rose to greatness with this enterprise, which soon acquired the character of an apostolic mission, for the spirit never entirely abandons the creations of matter. The pope divided all lands discovered or to be discovered between the two monarchies. The mediaeval crusade was succeeded by the crusade for America.

From Italy, whose mercantile genius almost matched the preeminence of her poetry, came map makers, more or less improvised, to place themselves at the disposition of these two crowns, and even of the English crown, which came very near losing out in the discovery of America. And in this atmosphere charged with potentialities, when it seemed anything could happen, there suddenly loomed the figure of Columbus, accompanied by the Pinzóns, those Dark Gods of the New World, who deserve more credit for the achievement than they are generally conceded.

Christopher Columbus was no isolated man, fallen providentially from heaven with an undivulged continent in his head. It is true that he used to speak of unknown lands "as though he carried them stored in a box," to quote Martín Alonso's graphic words. But he was not the first to mention them, nor did he, in this or in other matters, do anything else but pan the river of a secular tradition and find the golden sands. If we focus our attention on Columbus, we see a whole crowd of scholars and practical men, of the mad and the sane, who prepared him, helped him, and followed him. There can be but one objection to Carlyle's thesis of heroism in history, and that is, there are more heroes than are dreamed of in his philosophy. Let us, in justice, put a little order into this apotheosis, and disentangle the small roots that culminated in Columbus: some forerunners of October twelfth.

GEOGRAPHICAL MYSTICISM AND UNKNOWN COLONISTS

America may have received, in early times, informal visits which the world was not yet ready to take notice of, though they doubtless left their mark on the imagination. But here we must distinguish between the idea of discovery, strictly speaking, and the question of American origins, which is often erroneously confused with it, especially with regard to possible migrations across the Pacific.

We have referred to the mysticism of the West, man's vague urge to follow the sun's route to a point beyond where it shines on us. This strange magnetism of the West—"which past an illusion turns to East," as the poet says—pulsed through the oldest Mediterranean fables, and tantalized mediaeval fantasy with its mirage of fascinating islands, now paradisiacal, now—reversing the mirror—infernal. The Portuguese and other mariners sought them eagerly or shunned them in dread. They appeared, on the navigation charts of the fourteenth and fifteenth centuries, as tempting dots of color, and were the cause, in their dazzling deception, of shipwrecks, ill-conceived voyages, and chance discoveries; they were the obsession and the murmuration of the people.

As for involuntary Columbuses, the question has two aspects: the Pacific and the Atlantic. The former unravels into vague ethnic and linguistic conjectures; the latter seems to be boiled down to hoary sagas and the ingeniousness of some archaeologists. We are not so much concerned here with the quantum of proved truth as with the explosive power of fantasy.

It has been claimed that European travelers on the Atlantic had long been acquainted with the Isthmus of Panama as a crossing, and even with Cape Horn; that the travelers on the Pacific had regular itineraries for visiting the natural ports on the American coast. The haziness of these vagrant rumors is explained now by the imperfect contact between Asia and Europe, now by the jealousy of commerce, which concealed the sources of emeralds and gold. Secrets all the harder to keep, because a single voyage, a single adventure could create enormous wealth. It has been said that the hardships and long duration of these voyages made it necessary to found more or less permanent colonies. It has been maintained that proof of all this is afforded by evidence that the Peruvian Indians, before Pizarro—to judge by a certain textile of archaic weave discovered in a remote burial on the Island of the Moon, in Lake Titicaca—were already familiar with the European, the bearded one or "God-Man," and with the white woman, and with cows and horses as well, and even with the Biblical story of Adam and Eve and the forbidden fruit. According to this theory, the blend of Biblical legend and autochthonous myth that this textile clearly reveals is not a sign of the first rudimentary effects of Spanish catechism, but a sign of contact previous to the actual preaching of the gospel. This theory holds that the costumes of the figures pertain to the twelfth or thirteenth centuries. As though precision in dress could be looked for in a thing so rude! As if the mere fact that the warp of wool on cotton, in the style of Tiahuanacu, is not known to appear after the Conquest should rule out the survival of a few retarded specimens! To bolster the argument, the immaterial claim is made that the Incas, before the Conquest, had already begun to value silver and gold in the European fashion. Besides these tenuous theories, there are those concerning the so-called Cross of Palenque, which inspires vagaries of mysticism in some writers, and aberrations of history in others. Finally, proof is sought in some necklaces of Agri pearls found on mummies of the Pacific coast, and we are assured that such blue pearls must absolutely have been brought previous to the Discovery by Spanish or Venetian or Portuguese traders; that they were products of the Egyptian and Phoenician industry which left traces in Karnak, and flourished amazingly about the thirteenth century in Murano, Italy.

Other daring theories insist on the complicity of nature, as in the direction of currents, which are like rivers, "roads that move," though they move not on land but on the seas. The flow of wind and sea, according to these theories, could easily have caused unknown Columbuses to touch inadvertently on American shores. How often have ships left to themselves or badly steered, "drunken" ships, yielded to the slightest pressure and drifted off course! Thus, the junks of Japan, snatched away by storms, have come to die on the beaches of California. Thus, we are told, in the nineteenth century alone, more than fifteen Asiatic ships were cast up as wrecks on American shores. And whatever can be said of the black current, the Kuroshio, of the Pacific can be said also of the Atlantic, because of the different courses its waters take: the Equatorial stream, the Gulf Stream, the southern monsoons. Heredia, on a Welsh reef, could feel the aroma of his native Cuba wafted to him in mid-winter: "La fleur jadis eclose au jardin d'Amerique."

THE PACIFIC ROUTES. CHINESE IN AMERICA?

In 1761 a French Academician, de Guignes, stirred up a gale of controversy by attempting to show that the Fu-Sang of the Orientals was nothing else but the Mexico of the Europeans. The writer Ma-Twan-Lin tells that a certain Buddhist priest, returning from Fu-Sang in the year 499, describes that mysterious country in these words:

> The country Fu-Sang owes its name to its trees. These trees produce eatable sprouts, like those of the bamboo, and a savory red fruit. From the bark a fiber is taken for the manufacture of clothes. The inhabitants ride around in coaches drawn by horses, oxen, and deer. The oxen have strong horns, capable of supporting heavy burdens. The deer can be tamed, and the milk of the females is used to make cheese. There is an abundance of grapes; copper is found in great quantity, and nobody cares for silver or gold, because they are so plentiful. The houses are of wood, and—a strange thing—there are no walls around the cities. The inhabitants know how to write and manufacture a vegetable paper. They have neither armor nor lances, for they are very peaceable. The king's approach is heralded by bugles and drums, and he changes the color of his apparel according to the season of the year. There are only three classes of the nobility, which really does not amount to much. About 458, a mission of mendicants commenced to spread the true doctrine of the Buddha.

Opinion is unanimous, nowadays, that none of these traits apply to the New World. The growing of grapes, for instance, has been a tedious experiment which began (symbolically) with the frustrated attempts of Hidalgo, Father of Independence, and is beginning to become acclimated only in our day. Oxen and horses, as we know, were brought over by the Spaniards. The hieroglyphics of the imperial Aztec messengers represented oxen as "fat deer." And although there did exist a first American horse, in another era of palaeontology, not even a memory of it remains. Cortés could even play tricks with the terror that his horses inspired in the Indians.

After all, the possibility remains that there were casual landings by Asiatics on the shores of the Pacific, and even prehistoric communication, on the north, by way of Bering Strait. And as for that American Indian and that Mongolian who understood each other at once, when each was speaking his own language, this case has passed into the realm of folklore, although it may conceal a basis of truth. Newspapers have asserted that, a few years ago, an Oriental diplomat succeeded in tracing a linguistic affinity between a certain inscription that Mexican archaeologists were unable to read and some Mongolian dialect that had disappeared centuries ago. But this is only the latest version of the folkloric theme. And as for diplomatic missions between Aztecs and Orientals, much has been whispered and nothing proved aloud. The possible exotic origin of the Incas, across the western shores of South America, is still a matter of doubt.

There remains to be investigated the meaning of the affinities between the artistic products of the one people and the other, above all in the choice of color, and in the constructions of the final Inca phase, in which copper frames were used to hold together stone blocks. These things do not necessarily presuppose a contact between two peoples, but can be explained by the analogy of human reactions in the face of similar conditions (the Völkergedanke of Bastian). There remains to be investigated the significance of the evident ethnic similarities between Americans and Oceanians, but in any case we must go back here to an antiquity so remote, that the idea of discovery loses all meaning, and we are left only with the idea of racial origins.

THE ROUTES OF THE ATLANTIC:
THE SCANDINAVIANS IN AMERICA

Let us recall now the hypothesis of the unknown Columbuses of the Atlantic. In the form of tales and hoary rumors the tradition of this contact could easily have reached the Genoan.

The currents of the Atlantic establish three natural highways between the Old and the New World. One of them starts west of the British Isles or of Iceland and stops on the west coast of Greenland (for the east coast, heaped with ice, is not approachable), or else on the shores of Labrador or Newfoundland. The second, thanks to currents from the Canaries, and favored by the winds, leads to the Antilles. The third, cutting across the countercurrent from Guinea, by way of the Southern Equatorial, reaches Brazil, or else, making a detour by way of the Guianas, strikes the Lesser Antilles. The second route was the way Columbus came. The third was the way of Ojeda and Álvares Cabral, the discoverers of Brazil. And the first—is it not the same that Cortes-Real would one day follow? But, earlier, it could have been frequented by Normans, Basques, and Rochellois; and, still earlier, the Scandinavians seem to have traversed it.

The identification of the lands visited by Scandinavians has been a recent preoccupation. These lands were named Greenland, Helluland, Markland, and Vineland. Iceland had been touched upon as early as the eighth century by Irish and Scandinavians. In the following century, chance permitted a Norwegian pirate to discover it again. Those were the days of the lyrical sea, sailed almost at hazard; and leisure, as we know, is the fountainhead of investigation, in the same degree that necessity is.

Once Iceland was discovered, the highroad to the north was open to explorers. A couple of centuries later, the inhabitants of Iceland, the white land of frost, reached Greenland, which was given her name because of the color of the sea that bathes her shores, or, some say, according to other authorities, to entice covetous adventurers with the promise of lush forests. Here all names go by colors: the founder of Greenland is Erik the Red.

ACCORDING TO THE SAGA OF ERIK THE RED

These fierce pirates, it seems, founded no colonies, except Greenland, but were content to make rapid incursions. There is no use trying to follow their footsteps from the confused account given by the Northern Epic. It is possible, however, to draw some general inferences.

About the year 1000, a shipwreck gave the son of Erik the opportunity to tread that firm coast which would soon be known as Vineland. Between Newfoundland and Labrador, the explorers struck out through wooded regions teeming with game, till they reached a desolate cape, where they saw dunes and a rugged coastline that impressed them poetically, as something to marvel at.

Here, after the manner of Noah, when he loosed his birds from the Ark, they sent their Scottish runners Haki and Hekja, who were named for horses, to the interior, and the two returned after a time bringing spikelets of wheat and bunches of grapes, symbols of the soil's riches.

Farther to the south they found a great bay, and an island difficult of access, peopled by Negroes resembling the Africans, who navigated in boats of skins and were willing to exchange some articles with them. It seems they lived in caves, and their condition was primitive in the extreme.

From here on, it is impossible to find one's way in this labyrinth. There is a medley of dramatic and novelesque episodes that can not be trusted as history.

THE LEGENDARY SIGN

During the past century, historians who were determined to pinpoint the landing place of the Scandinavians believed they had found some signs on stones, as, for example, the celebrated rock of Dighton, on which an attempt had already been made to ascertain Phoenician or Siberian characters, but on which an Algonquin chief could recognize, finally, a simple Indian pictograph.

And then, it was the rock of Mohegan Island, on which were found some indecipherable marks, similar to runic signs, but these turned out to be natural abrasions.

On another occasion, Rafn believed he had found a Scandinavian monument, no less, at Newport, Rhode Island: a most singular round tower, which is, however, nothing more than the remains of a mill built by the governor of the island toward the end of the seventeenth century.

"No," some authorities say, "the Scandinavians never succeeded in establishing themselves on American soil, so they could hardly have left any lasting mark."

Others concede that the Normans navigated the Great Lakes

and ventured as far as the Mississippi Valley, and that runic stones in Minnesota and Kentucky remain as evidence.

The civilization of the Scandinavians in Greenland, which continued for three centuries, and sent forth at least two great expeditions to the American continent, went into a gradual decline, brought on by hostilities of the Eskimos. Greenland was already completely isolated from Europe in the fourteenth century, and her role henceforth was strictly that of the unknown; linked with other images borrowed from classical times, she served as an enticement for sailors, and as a bolster for the intimations of America's existence, and helped to bring about the second discovery in the sixteenth century.

FABLE, INSPIRATION, AND SCIENCE OF THE HUMANISTS

While geographical data and reports more or less verifiable contributed to the intimations of America, there were also conjectures of a purely imaginative type, which stemmed from the general excitement over voyages and discoveries.

Luigi Pulci, Italian poet of the Renaissance, has a story about a voyage that his characters Rinaldo and Ricciardotto made through the air, thanks to the demons Astarotte and Farfarello—forerunners of the Limping Devil of Spain, they obeyed the orders of Malagigi, the enchanter—and he puts into the mouth of Astarotte, ironic wit and freethinker, representing the new spirit of the age, the revelation that there exists a new world in the other hemisphere, situated beyond the Columns of Hercules, and inhabited, like the old. Rinaldo thereupon decides to seek that land, exploring the seas of Hercules, which, according to the traditional error, were supposed to be unnavigable, and fatal for men. (*Il Morgante Maggiore*, XXV, 228 ff.)

Is this prophecy to be considered mere poetic froth, like the well-known passage from Seneca's *Medea*? Or should it, rather, be considered the echo of an opinion already widespread, a fruit of the humanist culture?

Let us look farther. Although in speaking of the Renaissance there is a tendency to think only of the literary and artistic aspect of that immense revolution, we know that the "transvaluation of values," as it was called not long ago, far from being limited to the arts and letters, penetrated all human activity, transforming the whole idea of life. The fifteenth century was for Italy, and, in consequence, for the world, quite apart from its literary effervescence, a period of intense scientific preparation, even though the contribution of the humanists did make itself felt more impressively in the field of belles-lettres.

The times were not ready for anything more. Magic still held sway. Astrology flourished at court and was taught in the universities. And even the humanists, while they prepared, on one hand, the science of the future, paid tribute, on the other hand, to current superstitions. Even Pablo Toscanelli, representative man of science, who is known superlatively well to those versed in Columbian studies, through the discussions over his famous map, wasted a great deal of time in astrological vagaries, only to abandon them in his last years, when he became convinced that no constellation was favorable to him. What is said of astrology can be extended to magic, be it black magic or white or natural magic—a sort of sentimental physics, this last.

But, all in all, these groping experiments gathered in the seeds of the new science, which would repudiate the tottering errors of the Middle Ages.

OTHER GEOGRAPHICAL ANTECEDENTS

The all-embracing curiosity of the humanists, which made them universal men, did not disdain the study of geography. The incessant talk about voyages to faraway countries, about the lands of Prester John, about contrasting customs, tended, little by little, to banish the old dogmatic point of view. Even the writers of history did not dare to paint the exotic without breaking the accustomed molds and leaving off once and for all their habit of decking themselves out in remnants torn from the purple of Titus Livius. The Italians occupied an important place in nautical cartography before the fifteenth century and by then they had built a solid tradition in geography.

Mongol invasions in the thirteenth century had given rise to a movement of Christian missions which, although their aims were exclusively religious, contributed no little to knowledge of central and western Asia. In these missions there always went some Italian monks. And, as for the commercial voyagers, it is enough to recall Marco Polo, creator of modern Asiatic geography, who explored Asia longitudinally and discovered the wealth of China. Still other Italians, in those same years, reconnoitered the western coasts of Africa. Near the end of the fourteenth century, it seems, the Zeno brothers, Venetians, explored the northern Atlantic, and some time later Querini, also a Venetian, was shipwrecked on the far tip of Norway.

THE FERTILE ATLANTIS

The soil thus prepared was enriched, during the fifteenth century, with the fertilizer of classical culture. It was not long before the fruits began to show.

The studies of the ancients with regard to cosmography can be reduced to three chapters: (1) the roundness of the earth, (2) the antipodes, (3) the navigability of the ocean. The roundness of the earth was imagined, if not demonstrated, by the sages of Antiquity and transmitted to the Middle Ages in Arabic books. Among the Christians, some Fathers of the Church had disputed it, either through systematic opposition to Antiquity, or because they thought it incompatible with their own interpretation of the Bible. In Italy, it had been accepted—to cite only important names—by St. Thomas, Dante, Petrarch, Cecco d'Ascoli, and Fazio degli Uberti. Later, by Vinci and Toscanelli. Dante, loyal to the scholastics, considered the world of the antipodes uninhabited, "without people." This had also been the opinion of Isidore of Seville, of Lactantius, of St. Augustine. Already Petrarch believes in the ethnic antipodes, and already Pulci, who has brought us to these reflections, exclaims:

> Vedi che il sol di caminar s'affretta
> dove io ti dico che laggiu s'aspetta.

As for the third question, it was asserted that the same waters bathed the coasts of Spain and of India. (We are assured that one of Cicero's masters, Poseidon the Syrian, had foreseen the voyage to India by way of the West.) And the discussion, revived by the humanists, was prolonged in an effort to find out if an expansive or relatively small sea was concerned.

The humanists took to studying and translating Plato, Theopompus, Plutarch, Aristotle, Ptolemy, Strabo. And they found in them this notion of a land that had disappeared, called Atlantis, and this notion gradually began to acquire some credit.

The traditional story of Atlantis is taken up by Plato in his *Timaeus* and *Critias*, where he doubtless adapts it to his own taste. There are traces of this theme of a vast submerged island (which perhaps stems from the deluge) in the Greek legends as well as in the Nordic, in the Celtic as well as in the Arabic, and even, it seems, in the Mexican and in the Chinese, without there having been, necessarily, any single cataclysm that was responsible for them all. Plato, who here turns poet, describes for us the mighty empire founded by Poseidon, lord of the waters, a thalassocracy ruled by his descendants, the Ten Allied Kings. Superior to all other countries of her day, except old Athens, which was destined to triumph over the Atlantes; superior in her benign climate and in her fertile soil, in the richness of her metals, the magnificence of her temples, palaces, bridges and the general robustness of her structures; in the excellence of her sons and the learning of her institutions; the kingdom spread over a greater expanse than that of Asia and Africa as then known, a power that could reach with its conquests to the frontiers of Italy and Egypt. Today we cannot determine, in the jigsaw puzzle of earth and sea, exactly how to place the capricious shape of Atlantis, so vaguely described. Plato's story, assisted by ancient ideas about the configuration of the earth brought to light by the humanists, had a marked influence on explorers and cosmographers of the fifteenth century.

Meanwhile, America, sought now in all directions, became, before she was ever a proved fact, both a scientific and poetic intimation.

MILITANT HUMANISM

Nevertheless, for Ciriaco d'Ancona, the Italian humanists limited themselves to traveling through Italy and a part of Europe. But the land of their heart's desire they visited only in books.

What is important is that the travelers who were not humanists by profession seemed to move about at the express orders of the humanists. They performed, indeed, what others wrote, and thus came to constitute an actual militant humanism. Buondelmonti explored the Aegean, and remained for several years on Rhodes; it was from there, most likely, that he sent some Greek codices to Cosimo de' Medici. Niccolò de' Conti, a new Marco Polo, traveled through China and Indochina.

And here is a curious case: that of Ciriaco Pizzicolli d'Ancona, who, under the spell of humanism, left off being a trader and became a scholar; he went wandering through Italy, Greece, the Aegean, and Asia Minor, gathering documents. His voyages have a special importance because they show the first impulse, though vague as yet, to break through the circle of classical geography, to which the humanists so far had remained faithful.

And, of course, the influence of the humanists was already making itself felt in the business of map making. We see, in the nautical map of Becario (1435), to the southwest of Ireland, the famous island of "Brazil" and a certain "Antilles"—or "island placed in front"—which could be one of the Azores.

According to some students, Toscanelli and his drawings had an influence on Columbus's discovery. According to others, Columbus himself, in an attempt to give the enterprise a scientific basis, falsified all the documentation relating to these possible influences of Toscanelli. In any case, the atmosphere was full of ideas, and they all followed the direction that the humanists pointed out. The information given on Toscanelli's map appears also, for instance, on Martin Behaim's globe, with which Columbus had a great deal to do. In the works of Cardinal d'Ailly, and in those of Pius II as well, or in Marco Polo—three of Columbus's favorite authors—there are data referring to the existence of new lands across the ocean, and to the distance between Europe and Asia, which was supposed to be 130 degrees; navigation was made easy by intermediate islands, which permitted relays. Columbus, grounding himself on these authorities, calculated a figure for the circumference of the earth that was less than the real one by some ten million meters.

Add to these humanist notions the economic urgency that everyone was aware of: the need to find a sea lane for commerce to the Orient, dating from the conquest of Constantinople by the Turks; and add, even, the exasperation that was felt in the royal kitchens, deprived of tasty spices, for the mediaeval cuisine, although it aimed to please the eyes, dulled the palate with a surfeit of aromas. And from the sum of these things—and here we see the curious chain of history—we get the discovery of the Cape of Good Hope, and the discovery of the New World.

In this atmosphere, already charged with the necessary elements, the opportune hand of the wizard appears, makes a few passes in the air, catches and welds the glittering particles, and lo!—there in the palm of the hand is the shining coin.

THE LEGEND OF COLUMBUS

In the view of Francisco López de Gómara, the discovery of America was "the most important thing that has happened since the creation of the world, save only the incarnation and death of Him who created it." This point of view, which has been adopted by many since Gómara, while it reveals an astonishment that is perfectly legitimate, is equivalent to opening the eyes extremely wide. But, as we know, this is no way to see better. On the contrary. Eyes opened extremely wide are the eyes of hallucination and of ecstasy. They engender, in themselves, the phantasms of legend.

A profuse and uncultivated vegetation grows around the memory of the Genoan. In order to arrive at Christopher Columbus, we must hew a path through overgrowth. It would seem that Columbus made a special effort to place himself beyond the reach of history, or else that the grandeur of his deed stifled investigation to the same degree that it aroused admiration. History tries in vain to impose its precise measurements. Legend, torn to pieces a hundred times, recovers its vitality again and again, like rue crushed underfoot. This happens because the instinct of the people, when they contemplate their favorite heroes, is not content with the tribute offered by logical truth. So they must invent sacrifice, with its double aspect of anguish and art. Hence the tales of supernatural greatness and of martyrdom undeserved, the *sparagmos* and the deification of the Greek demigods.

We discover, on all sides, around the figure of Christopher Columbus, inaccuracies that are perpetuated with loving care. Legend was already ripe in the days of Fray Bartolomé de las Casas, is still flourishing today, and is transmitted in school textbooks. The process of purification, which began with Alexander von Humboldt, reaches the most paradoxical conclusions in our time. And thus, while for some writers Columbus is inspired and spotless, the unimpeachable and persecuted sage, for others he is a brazen scoundrel: like those busybodies who, unable to make

a place for themselves in their own country, "go elsewhere to
sell their thread," he went from court to court as a swindler,
perpetrating fraud or at the very least mad schemes, which he
never suspected would later turn out to be sound. He was neither
the one nor the other. In vain did the poetic genius of Paul
Claudel, invoking the combined resources of theater and cinema,
attempt a reconciliation of these two extremes. We must resign
ourselves to human nature, "diverse and wavering."

The legend of Columbus has long provided a theme for
painters of historical subjects. Who does not recall, as a familiar
scene, the Catholic Queen handing over the precious jewels to
Columbus? The subject offers an excuse for a veritable debauch
of furniture, costumes, antique tapestries. The kneeling figure of
Columbus receiving the coffer of treasure from Isabella is en-
graved on the sentimental retina. It belongs to the home and to
infancy and to the family; it is confused amongst earliest memories. Let no one take it away! No matter how unauthentic, this is,
at the very least, a symbolization that sharpens our understanding
of history, because it suggests the very real division of Spanish
affairs of state in those times: Ferdinand for the interior, Isabella
for the exterior. King Ferdinand governed the court, interweaving the ambitions of the courtiers, balancing forces with the
brilliance and subtlety that Gracián ascribes to him; Queen Isabella, our Isabella, dreamed of giving wings to the Spanish virtue,
in the form of lances on earth and sails on the sea. Striking contrast between Aragon and Castile.

From motives more puerile than patriotic, someone will insist,
from time to time, on reviving discussions that are definitively
settled, and each year we must decide once again whether
Columbus was a descendant of expelled Jews, or whether he was
a Galician born in Pontevedra, or even a Catalonian. The linguistic arguments, fortunately, are beside the point: Columbus
spoke and wrote the gibberish of those who, trained in colloquial
talk and not in written language, leave their own people while
still young and must learn very fast to carry on in different
tongues in order to earn their livelihood. Columbus used, when
it suited his convenience, commercial Latin or "Genovisco," the
Portuguese of the streets, and Spanish of the finest strain, the first
modern language that he wrote in, although with some admixture
of Portuguese. For Spain was to be the country of his choice, in

the end, the country from which he hoped to obtain benefits and rewards.

THE HISTORY OF COLUMBUS

We shall ignore the illustrious parentage with which he later tried to endow himself, nor do we have to believe that he was occupied from boyhood with the business of war and of the sea. After success came falsification, first in matters of science and then in personal history. This man of providence fortified himself with theoretical excuses, and forged for himself grandfathers of high lineage, and he may have used for this purpose facts out of his own life, in order to hide something base or even damaging in his background.

A wool dealer of Genoa and Savona, son of a modest family of weavers in which there had never been a sailor, at the age of twenty-odd he was still practicing his hereditary trade at home, according to the wisdom of the poor. He never acquired much knowledge of the mysteries of mathematics or cosmography, and most likely knew only by hearsay some of the authors that he mentions. And the truth is, if his erudition was often second-hand, the fact takes nothing from his stature. Neither did he know how to measure a degree of the earth (but generals are not required to point the cannon with their own hands), nor did he serve as a child under the orders of the good King René, nor under the command of those admirals nicknamed—but not named—Colombos (or "Doves"), and they were not even Italians. One day, while traveling, perhaps in the commerce of cloth, he was forced to land in Portugal; he went on to England, but then returned to live among the Portuguese, right in the valiant hatchery of all the geographic dreams. Married to the daughter of Perestrello, a navigator full of curiosity and information, he began to rub elbows with sailor folk and to feel like a sailor himself. And if he did not succeed in becoming the most expert of cosmographers, neither was he the worst. Oh, what an appetite he had for bits of news! He listened to everything that was said in the gossip shops of the port, and to the tales of old sea dogs; he mingled with the human surf that eddied in the taverns, and babbled about the miracles of the sea.

Perhaps he had begun then to revolve his project in his mind;

it may have already been formulated by 1482. Some claim that this primitive project had nothing to do with opening a new route to the East by way of the West. That, grounding himself on copious information bequeathed to him by his father-in-law, on the sayings of ancient mariners, on letters now lost, on memories of shipwrecks—in sum, on data more or less reliable, mixed with the folklore of the sea—Columbus was trying to find nothing less than a new land, the Antilles of the fabulous tales, although he took good care not to say so, in order not to alarm people, or in order not to betray his secret.

DOUBT IN THE MIDDLE OF THE SEA: DUEL BETWEEN THE ANTILLES AND CIPANGO

According to this hypothesis, which I shall set out objectively, without judging it, the enterprise that ended as a success began as a prodigious double delusion.

The only real support that Columbus could count on, besides the moral backing of the Catholic Kings, was that of the ship-outfitter Martín Alonso Pinzón. He had heard in Rome of the mysterious island of Cipango, which could be found on the way to Asia, and he dreamed of discovering it. He advised Columbus not talk about his new lands any more; such tales were badly discredited; if he wanted to recruit men and to keep his standing at court, he should put emphasis on the new route to Asia.

Columbus, to be forearmed, asked for and received credentials introducing him to the great Khan, asked for and received an appointment as viceroy of any new lands he might find. And together they put to sea: Columbus in search of his Antilles and Pinzón in search of his Cipango. But if the route of the ships was the same, the voyage that each man was making in his own mind was different. And not until they were 750 leagues from the Canaries, without having sighted land, did Columbus, disappointed, begin to have doubts. The Antilles were nowhere to be seen, so there was no alternative but to look for the island of Cipango.

This notable turning point in the doctrine of the Discovery was reached, according to the hypothesis that I am following, precisely on October 6, 1492. Martín Alonso took advantage of his Genoese partner's dismay and persuaded him to change course, abandoning the twenty-eighth parallel and veering a little to the southwest. When the flight of birds announced land, Columbus had to accept the definitive reform of his first plan. This, he must have thought, was not his Antilles, the Antilles he had secretly cherished until now. And he then adopted the other man's delusion as his own, and died believing he had discovered a new route to India.

If this hypothesis is sound, nothing could be more intriguing than this double delusion, a jewel with two facets; either Columbus discovered a new world by the merest chance, or else, damned for lack of faith, he died in error, even anxious to apologize for the very success he had hoped for.

If the Discovery is viewed thus, as a transcendental duel between Japan and Haiti, between Cipango and the Antilles, in which the Antilles disguised themselves as Cipango in order to triumph in the end; as a semi-geographical or semi-fabulous dispute between Pinzón and Columbus, aboard a couple of caravels in the middle of an unknown sea—does it not take on a higher sense of drama? Imagine the bold mariners nervously scrutinizing their maps, turning the compass chart about, interrogating the sea and sky, looking each other fixedly in the eye, as if each would like to catch sight of the sought-for land in the eyes of the other. In that instant, the New World quivered on the horizon.

A LITTLE COMEDY ABOUT COLUMBUS

Let us try to re-create, in a sort of play, with the aid of trustworthy evidence and a dash of imagination, one of the crucial moments of this voyage, in order that the meaning may stand out as in bold letters from the tangled script.

On a day in October, 1492, Martín Alonso Pinzón, sailing on the *Pinta*, which was in the lead, either because it was the fastest or because he was the most expert sailor, stopped the ship, waited for Columbus to catch up with him on the *Santa María*, and called him to his side for a conference, alone and without witnesses. The conversation that they had then upset previous ideas.

"You are determined, Christopher, to discover a new land. This is why your plans won small credit among monarchs and scholars, who had to be virtually taken by assault before we could get as far as we have."

"It is a rule of prudence that great enterprises should never be easy to start."

"I know perfectly well you are talking about the Antilles, although you conceal the fact with great care. But the Antilles you dream about exist only in those silly stories that have turned your head, or in those damned papers of your father-in-law's that you hide from the gaze of the curious. You are new to this business; you don't have it in your blood, as I do, by family inheritance. You can still be taken in by old wives' tales. If you had set out from the beginning, as I have explained to you often enough, instead of hatching these fantastic plans, to discover the new route to Cipango—that island of clotted gold which lies toward the eastern Indies, and which we are bound to reach by sailing always to the west, if my information is correct—I guarantee you would have long ago reached your goal."

"Alonso, you are the only man who can talk to me in an admonitory tone, for I consider you my master and my loyal friend. I am not, certainly, a sailor from several generations back, but the son of humble weavers. Nor am I a Corsican, nor is it worthwhile to ask if I am a Spanish Jew, as rumor now insists. I have revealed to you already, for you are my true partner, who will share my risks and my luck, that those admirals who were called Colombos, and to whom I claim kin when faced with the sort that can accept the truth only when it is served to them with a garnish of fiction, were never any kin of mine, nor were they called Colombos except as a nickname, nor were they even Italians. One of them, George de Bissipat, was Greek; another, William de Casenove, was French. With none of them did I sail the sea, and much less under the orders of King René. Nor do I have any connection with the Counts of Placencia. Nor did I follow a course of studies at Pavia, nor did I ever go to any school except the weaving shop of my father, apart from the school that my own ambition provided for me later on. And the truth is, if I had not been shipwrecked, as you know, on a voyage to England with a cargo of cloth and Genoese knickknacks, I would never have arrived in Portugal or married the daughter of Perestrello, and my head would never have been turned, as you put it, by all those stories and all those papers. But as you know very well, while I may pretend to greater erudition than I possess, when among those doctors who pride themselves so on citations and footnotes, I have studied assiduously some stores of wisdom that are easily worth any number of books . . ."

"Nothing could be farther from my mind than to belittle your genius or your attainments."

"Anyone who, like yourself, has learned so much about the world from his own dealings with it, can hardly tax me with not being equal to my project, for we all know that very great deeds have humble beginnings, and a persevering will is worth more than any amount of meditation. It is not for men of my nature to burn themselves out in quiet studies, but to put these studies boldly to the test for the benefit of all and find out what is valid in them."

"As you can see very well, I return your trust. But I find it hard to believe that you could fall into those lunacies about the Antilles."

"Do I have to explain it to you all over again? Papers, books, conversations of experts, the reports I gathered during my short visit to Guinea—does all that seem like lunacy to you? How else does anyone acquire information? Was not this the way Porto-Santo was discovered, and Madera? I tell you, there is still much land to be discovered west of the Canary Islands and of Cape Verde, and there we will come upon the Antilles where, in times past, the persecuted Portuguese found refuge, and the Isle of the Seven Cities which the old maps show, as does the globe of Behaim. And if I have dissembled my hopes, I have done so on your advice, and to my own misfortune. You know what happened with King John. It was not because my venture was too reckless, for he did not judge it to be so, but because of the price I put on it, that he delayed carrying it out, while he prepared a secret expedition, to rob me of my own. And now it is my turn to ask you: What is there about your Cipango that makes it any better than my Antilles?"

"You are not unacquainted, Christopher, with the many and sound writings on Cipango; and you will remember that, when the padres of the convent at Rábida sent you to me, you had to wait for me to return from Rome, where, besides attending to some profitable deals, which is always a good thing to do, I was getting news from Cipango with the help of a scholar in the

Vatican Library. I heard also, I must confess, of some islands that I would run into on the way, and one of them might be your Antilles."

"That is why we were able to reach an agreement."

"And for that reason I promised you and gave you the material means for the enterprise (you know full well great lords are not to be trusted, even if they are called Medinaceli or something still higher than the sky), on the condition that you would agree to keep going until we reached Cipango."

"And for that reason, Alonso, at the same time I asked to be named viceroy of any new lands that were discovered, I agreed to carry with me, in order to satisfy you, the Royal Letter for the Great Khan of India, if we should actually arrive in his kingdom."

"And I, for my part, confessed to you that, if you had delayed any longer, I would have taken to sea by myself. That I had already made notes, more than a few, on the maps by Pizzigano, by Becaria, by Bianco, by Jareto, and by Benincasa, which show these islands. And I tell you again, we should have got this business started earlier, even though the Court was preoccupied with the Moors, if, instead of promising new lands, which you were in the habit of talking about as though you carried them stored in a box, you had simply promised instead new and shorter roads to the wealth already known."

"It is true, Alonso, that you have taken it upon yourself to recruit the men and arm the expedition in Palos, where I was ignored as a foreigner. And it was not from fear of the Shadowy Sea, which served very well to frighten people in the days of Don Enrique, that they balked at coming aboard, but because they had little or no faith in me."

"And also, Christopher, because they suspected you were going to look for the Antilles, and the Portuguese had already come to grief in these searches, and the people of Palos knew this. It was then that I decided to assist you with all my family, brothers, resources. And I had to convince everyone that we were going to look for Cipango, and not the Antilles, promising them houses roofed with gold, which is what I truly expect to find. But now, just between you and me, and with the greatest love, I admonish you. I am all yours, and loyal, and I have no intention of asking any return for the services that you acknowledge, and I always address you, when there are witnesses, with the full respect that is proper for the best conduct of the king's government, and you, indeed, are his officer, and with the respect that I owe you because of the friendship I profess."

"Unburden yourself, Alonso: I have always listened to you."

"Well, then, this is what has happened: ever since we put to sea we have gone from blunder to blunder so you could hold with your obsession. You ordered us to sail on the same parallel, as we have done. On the seventeenth of September, when we were more than 400 leagues out from the Canaries, you ordered me to search for an island that did not exist: no doubt, one more fiction we owe to Perestrello and his famous papers. Afterward, we crossed that sea full of weeds that Vásquez de la Frontera told you about, and there, on the twenty-fourth, as stated in your diary, the hoped-for islands eluded us again. And, finally, we arrived at the limit of 750 leagues, where, in an access of enthusiasm, you promised the men we would find land. And, pardon me for reminding you of this, but if I had not put my ship crosswise when the uproar was at its height, and shouted my advice to hang a half dozen scoundrels and toss them into the sea, the men of the *Santa María* would have made an end of you and your ambitious plans. That human ballast now refuses to sail on indefinitely, fearing that the wind, favorable so far, will make the return trip difficult. I have to tell them every minute there will be no Palos if there is no Cipango, and I will not return without the land that I go to seek. On the seventh of October I persuaded you to veer to the southwest, and now you can see by the flight of birds, land cannot be far off."

"Whether it is my Antilles or your Cipango, I do not know myself any more. But I still think that we could very easily strike the land I am looking for, in spite of the diversion to the Southwest, for it is so extensive, it must stretch to the extremes of north and south."

"Do not go on like this, or they will take you for a lunatic; resign yourself to the truth. Marco Polo, whose works you have studied, says that Cipango is situated 1,500 lis from India, which means it cannot be far away now."

"Let there be land; it makes no difference what land. As for myself, at the moment I cannot overcome my dreams and imaginings, and think I see before me a vast unknown kingdom.

But should the time come, I shall bring out my letter and put away my viceregality. I am, then, an ambassador who arrives by an unexplored route at a well-known country."

"As plain and as true as the chain there, that the lady Felipa Moñiz hung around your neck."

"God forgive me! When I put on this chain, the daughter of Perestrello did not even exist. This chain was clasped about me by that Cordovan woman. I told you all about it. Her name was Beatrice Enriquez. God forgive me!"

Suddenly there is an uproar; shouts are heard; bursting wildly into the cabin comes the cosmographer Juan de la Cosa, captain and owner of the *Santa María*, with the pilots Bartolome Roldán and Sancho Ruiz; the pilots of the *Pinta*, Francisco Martín Pinzón and Cristobal Garcia Sarmiento; and the youth Vicente Yáñez Pinzón, captain of the *Niña*, followed by his pilot Pero Niño.

Martín Alonso speaks:

"No need to say anything, gentlemen: I see it on your faces. Don Christopher, Lord Admiral: you have touched land, and have discovered the western way to the East Indies that you promised to the world."

INSIDE COLUMBUS'S HEAD

It is not essential that we accept this hypothesis, ingenious though it is, which I have been outlining and dramatizing, in order to realize that the origins of the Discovery contain a powerful element of myth. For a better view of this element, we must, in a manner of speaking, go inside the head of the Discoverer.

We have, on one hand, the glimmerings of fact that Columbus had collected from the news brought by travelers and adventurers who by chance had touched upon unknown lands or seen them from a distance. Oviedo and Garcilaso the Inca tell us how the shipwrecked Alonso Sánchez de Huelva came to Columbus's house to die, bequeathing to him in gratitude his documents and notes. The pilot, Pedro Velasco, in La Rábida, gave Columbus the approximate route to the Island of Flowers, 150 leagues from Fayal. The one-eyed man of Santa Maria and the Galician of Murcia talked about the ships that struck on Newfoundland or Bacaláos. A certain sailor of Murcia, whose accounts seemed much like hallucinations, swore that he had described unexplored lands on every voyage. And Vásquez de la Frontera, sailing in the service of Portugal, had also reported some glimpses. In order to evaluate this more or less vague evidence, we must remember that these old sailors and pilots navigated as traders, not discoverers; what was important to them was not the glory of science, but the secret of possible profits; so they preferred to conceal their knowledge or their conjectures. Columbus came to them already inspired by the humanists of the Mediterranean with the longing to discover and to propagate the fruits of discovery, to build upon geographical discovery not only, if possible, a private fortune, but also an enrichment of human life in general.

But let use set this murky evidence aside, likewise the erratic calculations of distance between lands known and unknown. Let us give our attention solely to what was imaginary and impossible among Columbus's notions. It is really an edifying picture.

Whether Toscanelli's map was forged, or whether it was authentic, it is proof that Columbus was obsessed by the lands described by Marco Polo. It is from *Il Milione*, indeed, that he got those displaced cities of marble, gold, silver, and precious stones, reflected in majestic streams, and the idea of that dazzling Cathay which the Middle Ages filled with monsters and dragons. The *Historia Rerum* of Pius II provided Columbus with material for still more dreams and imaginings; and Cardinal d'Ailly filled his fancy with griffins, dragons, basilisks, unicorns, many-headed serpents, gargoyles and chimeras, and other freaks that were crosses between two species and relics of classical antiquity or of the mediaeval bestiaries; figures from a zoological hell in which there were nevertheless a few handsome creations, like the phoenix—as old as Herodotus—which is reborn from its ashes.

The classical Utopia of the Golden Age had little by little turned into the dream of an earthly paradise. The idea that a kingdom of happiness exists, where all men are naturally good— a faraway foreshadowing of Rousseau's philosophical dream— flourished on all sides. If some thought Cathay was a hatchery of hellish creatures, others thought it was Eden itself. Mandeville, Marco Polo, Christine de Pisán made this last belief popular. The notion that the noble savage is a man covered with long hair, a point that was still being gravely discussed by scholars in the eighteenth century, and that inspired the disguises worn at the famous Dance of the Burning under Carlos V, was derived from Dionysius of Halicarnassus and passed on from one author to another. Brunetto Latini, who was Dante's teacher, contributed his share to the proliferation of so-called unknown lands. And Cardinal d'Ailly, who was for Columbus the highest authority, believed in the existence of a most blissful people, living far to the north, almost immortal, so surfeited with happiness and long life, some of them would commit suicide; he also believed in giant pygmies and in Macrobees with the body of a lion and the talons of an eagle. According to him, there were men who ate raw fish and drank only sea water, and there were men who howled like dogs instead of articulating words; there were cyclops; there were amazons; there were those who had but one foot, which served as a parasol when they slept; there were men without heads and others with eyes in the nape of the neck; and there were the gentle dwellers on the banks of the Ganges, who died at the slightest whiff of a bad smell and who fed on the aromas of fruits.

Columbus, prepared by these writings, set out on his voyage, and it is hardly surprising that, in his mind, fabulous visions often usurped the place of reality, as his own narrative of his adventures reveals in every part. He could, for instance, have left us a realistic impression of life and nature in America. But no: he lets fable stand in the way; his desire to find here the confirmation of his mythological prejudices deprives us of any description that can be compared to his highly vivid description of the storms at sea.

It even seems that this mystical obsession grew on him between the first and fourth voyages, as if, at the beginning, the very grandeur of the deed kept him in a somewhat humble and expectant attitude. But then he let his subjective audacity go always farther and farther, giving himself over to airy interpretations, and showing less and less reserve in identifying the places he found with the names he had learned in books.

We have already seen what roles the myths of Cipango and of the Antilles may have played in the ideology of the first voyage. But other elements of myth were not lacking on that journey, beginning with the uncertainty that has persisted with regard to the first island of the Lucayas (Bahamas) touched upon by the discoverers. Columbus, during the three months that he explored the Antilles, suspected—amidst those trees and naked men—that he may have found the Biblical Eden, that he might find farther on the immensely wealthy countries that Marco Polo had promised him. . . . He wants to impose his fantasy on the real object, and he does not mind twisting the shape of the truth a little in order to make it conform to his expectations. Cipango, the country of the Anthropophagi, the kingdom of the Amazons flee like mischievous sprites before his keel, leaving him behind on one island after another.

The Caribbean group, which Columbus explored on his second voyage, became, in the popular imagination, the land of the Polyphemes and Lestrigones, according to Peter Martyr. As for the Spanish Island, or Hispaniola, the island of Santo Domingo, shaped like a chestnut leaf, notes Peter Martyr—it was immediately confused, in the Admiral's eyes, with the land of Ophir, from whence came the riches that the Old Testament attributes to Solomon, king of Jerusalem: gold, sandalwood, and precious stones.

On the third voyage—Columbus's report of it has been called "the work of one possessed"—he was seeking Cochin-China, Malacca, the golden Cheresonese, Taprobane; and when he came upon the mouths of the Orinoco, he declared it to be his firm conviction that he was approaching the vicinity of Paradise, and that only an inopportune illness prevented him from reaching it.

On the fourth voyage he is talking like a visionary, like a man with hallucinations. He snatches the maps from his men so that no one will know which way he is heading. The idea of a divine mission begins to get mixed with his geographical chimera. Before he took ship, Columbus had offered his services to the Pope for the conquest of the Holy Sepulchre. And now this great discoverer of a new world is losing touch with the world. In some of his reports he tells of having received supernatural messages: he has heard voices, in the manner of the chosen and the prophets. Humboldt will even pose the question whether these letters of the last voyage do not already reveal the beginnings of mental illness.

The foregoing picture, it seems to me, is edifying because it proves the power of a mirage. A bit of exaggeration, a hint of caricature, surely, will not offend the decorum of history: let us dare to say that the discovery of America was the result of failures in science, and of triumphs in poetry.

COLUMBUS'S BAD LUCK

There is a disconcerting aspect of the legendary transfiguration of Columbus. The very enthusiasm that exalts the Admiral decrees infamy for all his companions.

There were some among them like Juan de la Cosa, a "master Map maker," who would later be the discoverer of Venezuela, and whose maps were regarded by Peter Martyr as among the most recommendable, and who was the first to draw the shore line of Venezuela, and the first to realize that Cuba was an island. Later on he would describe for us his exploration of the coasts of Panama and Colombia. There is some confusion about his last voyages, for it seems that, he was in the habit of tracing all his wanderings over the earth on charts, yet he neglected to describe them. Even the personal identity of this "Juan de la Cosa, the Basque" had suffered from the suspicions of scholars, for some of them have tried to divide him in two, as certain critics have done with Homer, setting to one side Juan de la Cosa, and to the other, Juan the Basque. To those who think they were one and the same, the partition seems as absurd as selling a cat and charging separately for the tail.

In any case, Juan de la Cosa was captain and owner of the *Santa María*, and considering his reputation as a map maker and the authority that he had on the first voyage, it would not be surprising if he had discussed a few points of navigation with the Admiral, or if he had learned a few things from him, or even a good many things. Columbus himself sailed aboard the *Santa María*—which later was lost on the coast of Santo Domingo— and it seems from documents of the times that he was continually making charts and calculations, and that he "plotted the routes with Cosa." Apparently, also, Columbus would upbraid his servants Salcedo and Ayal for sharing the secret maps with the Basque. Discord, although surreptitious as yet, and contraband, nevertheless went along in the caravels of the Discovery.

The return trip was no longer a voyage of eager captains, inspired by an ideal, but of men filled with greed and mutual distrust.

And if the annual glorifications of Columbus have forgotten the modest Juan de la Cosa, each year we hear once again curses on Martín Alonso Pinzón, the good navigator, whose crime consists of having shown, as an expert, some degree of impatience, and of having sailed in the *Pinta,* which was faster than the *Nina* and the *Santa María.*

And what do they say about the amiable Florentine, Amerigo Vespucci? That his voyages were imaginary; that he tried to steal Columbus's daughter; that, ambitious, he succeeded in giving his name to something he had no claim to whatsoever, and, finally, that America should have been called Columbia—a contention that nobody would oppose, if it were not too late. As if Vespucci were to blame because posterity gained, through his narratives, a better understanding of the voyages of Columbus, and even of the subsequent voyages of Juan de la Cosa, whether he really took part in all that he tells about or not! He owes his destiny to his good pen, nothing more.

Columbus possessed the creative drive of cosmic forces. At first glance, he is one of those enterprising, cosmopolitan Italians with something of the wild-eyed speculator in them, and with no capital except their inspiration, who, not without grossness and madness, batter down the obstacles in their way, half poet, half wizard, confused and combative, rash and unruly, discontented dissemblers, tenacious visionaries, full of effective insults, at once mean and sublime. But, on final inspection, when we look at his achievement, he turns out to be the Hero, the romantic animal of destiny. And we find, in this Hero's company, a number of the discreet, who took it upon themselves to hold his inspired audacities in check, and to guide the essentially sterile spirit into ways of practical reality. The map maker Juan de la Cosa, the narrator Amerigo Vespucci, the ship-outfitters known as the Pinzóns, together made the success of the enterprise possible and even inevitable, by contributing their opportune and understanding corrections, and the written expression that helps us view the Discovery with insight, whether we look upon it as an exploit, or as the theme of literature.

EPISTLE TO THE PINZÓNS

Martín Alonso, Vicente Yáñez, Francisco Martín:
Your private quarrels with Christopher Columbus do not affect
America's gratitude. Especially since Martín Alonso died on his
return from the first voyage, and had no chance to defend himself. Your personal failings do not concern history. The possible
confusion of identities among you makes it even harder to reach
a verdict, and we must suspend judgment on a case that we really
know nothing about. We can not tell for certain whether it was
Martín Alonso or Francisco Martín who went as lieutenant on
the supposed expedition of the Frenchman Jean Cousin, which,
some say, put to sea at Dieppe, under the guidance of the master
pilot Father Descaliers, and got as far as the mouth of the
Amazon, where it turned toward Africa and passed Point Aduja,
already touched upon by Bartolomé Díaz. Some say that it was
Martín Alonso who committed a disloyal act, provoking a mutiny
on board ship against his captain in an attempt to snatch the glory
of the enterprise from him, and that he was tried for this on his
return by the maritime court and sentenced to lose his honors
and privileges and exiled forever from the service of the city.
And they account in this way for the firmness that Martín
Alonso showed when he succeeded in calming Columbus's muti-
nous crew, like a man who already felt at home in those waters,
and for the assurance with which he advised a turn to the southwest—which may have resulted in their reaching the island of
San Salvador instead of Florida—and even for his act of dis-
obedience, when he stole away from Columbus, leaving him in
Cuba, and spent forty-five days on a fruitless search for the route
to the Amazon, which had already been found. What we do
know is that the moment land hove in sight, land that Martín
Pinzón's caravel, the lead ship, was first to see, his defects began
to show: his jealousy of the improvised admiral who outranked
him, his ambition to be known as the true discoverer. What we
do know is that, on the return trip, in spite of damage to the
Pinta, Martín Alonso made every possible effort—even blessing
the sea when it turned rough—to arrive first with tidings of the
newly discovered lands, and thus win the first rewards. All in
vain, because Columbus managed to come in ahead of him. It has

been alleged, besides, that Vicente Yáñez had sinister designs, even though he never left Columbus's side. But nothing can erase the proved deeds and facts of the coöperation of the Pinzóns, which was decisive.

Your fate, Pinzóns, has been truly hard! You dreamed all your lives of becoming discoverers; you were professional mariners; you embarked on every famous expedition of your time, risking your credit, money, family, and lives, and yet not one of you is known as the discoverer of a single island. The fate of Martín Alonso was to make way for Columbus. As for Vincente Yáñez, who, in 1500, with four caravels reached the Cape of Santa María de la Consolación (which may be San Agustín or Macusipe or Cabo Norte), and, following the coast of Brazil, placed landmarks, witnessed the *pororoca*, or bore of the Marañon at the mouth of the Mearim, and entered as far as the delta of the Amazon—he had to make way for Cabral, who was not a navigator either, and who likewise discovered Brazil by accident, three months later.

What we must bear in mind is that Martín Alonso was a rich seafarer, with a reputation for skill and reliability and not a foreign interloper who could hardly inspire confidence. He was one of a large, well-known and honorable family. He was an intellectual, on cordial terms with the scholars of Rome, and, when the occasion required, a man of action, as he proved in battles with the Portuguese. Two of the three caravels in the Discovery were his. It was thanks to his personal influence that his brothers and Juan de la Cosa, all mariners with experience and skill, decided to help Columbus. A third of the money for the expedition came out of his own pocket. And, finally, without his sponsorship it would not have been possible to recruit men for the voyage. We know for a fact that, before he joined Columbus, not a single sailor was available, in spite of the royal decree granting a pardon to any prisoner who would enlist.

Once the agreement between the Crown and Columbus had been signed, the city of Palos, an important center for overseas trade, was ordered to furnish two caravels at its own expense. Why this order? We learn from the royal decree that this command was part of a sentence which, "for the commission of certain illegal acts," condemned the city of Palos to provide the service of the king with two armed caravels for a year. This, then, was a demand that a penalty be paid, and was by no means a generous offer on the part of the monarch. But the city of Palos ignored the order, and Columbus began to feel he had been abandoned. Then the *Pinta* was impounded by royal officers of Castile and turned over to Columbus. But what could he do with a ship that had no equipment and no supplies? To Columbus it seemed an insult. Then the Franciscan friar Juan Pérez came to his aid; and the aid consisted, simply, in persuading the Pinzón brothers to join the enterprise. And, without them, the royal decree, the protection of the Duke of Medinaceli, and the favor of Marchena would have availed nothing.

From this moment everything changed. Men offered their services. Supplies were found: food, arms, medicines, sails, rigging, and the water needed for a long voyage. And the expedition was ready to sail in a few weeks. The *Pinta* was no longer a ship seized by force but one voluntarily turned over. Vincente Yáñez contributed the *Nina*, and Juan de la Cosa, the *Calega*, which was now called the *Santa María*. Between Palos and La Róbida there was a steady stream of people coming and going. Besides the three Pinzón brothers, three more members of the family announced their intention to embark: Martín Alonso's son, Arias Martín, Diego Martín the elder, and Bartholomé Martín, his son. Did the Pinzóns ask too much when they wanted a little of the gain and the glory? Martín Alonso's authority still makes itself felt in the testimony of his trial, held twenty years after his death. And it certainly made itself felt in his lifetime, in a most impressive way, on the occasion of the mutiny on board, which grew out of the terror inspired by the deviation of the compass as they approached the Equator—a mutiny that might have put an end to the whole business, and that neither Columbus nor the practical Juan de la Cosa was able to cope with unaided. Columbus was the admiral; Martín Alonso the administrator. The former was the leader; the latter the technician. This duality, although discord was built into it from the start, was nevertheless what made the Discovery possible: the spark of a dream had fallen on the dry powder of reality. And the Discovery, like all the great Iberian achievements, was in good measure the work of private initiative.

It was private initiative that provided the decisive power in the reconquest of Spain from the Moors; and the hero who symbolizes this initiative was the Cid, an "outlaw" or "outcast" exiled by the king; the Cid Campeador, the "Warrior Chief," who was barred by the sovereign's order from all the inns of Burgos; who obtained the money he needed by leaving as security a chest full of pebbles; who recruited his fighting men among the destitute and the desperate; who captured, at his own cost and risk, the cities of Castejón, Alcocer, and Poyo de Monreal, and raided the lands of Alcañiz and those of the Count of Barcelona, and took Murviedro and Puig, and finally, always on his own authority, made himself master of Valencia. And still he allowed himself, from time to time, the luxury of sending gifts to the monarch: fine horses with fancy trappings, as a vainglorious gesture, in part, but also, in part, as a sign of staunch fealty. For the individualism of the Spaniard was not anarchic, nor was it rancorous.

For a while it seemed that private initiative had ascended the throne—if a paradox may be excused for the sake of brevity— in the persons of the Catholic monarchs; and the monarchy, national and home-grown, was gradually bringing the kingdom to a degree of unity. But Ferdinand and Isabella were cursed with feeble successors, and the foreign dynasties that came afterward either deviated from the direction of Spanish life to such an extent that the divergence became ever wider with time, or they failed to establish links between Spain and the rest of Europe.

In the Discovery, Pinzóns, the private initiative was yours. In the Conquest, it belonged to Hernán Cortés, who began by shaking off the authority of Diego Velásquez and dashing into Mexico on his own responsibility. And the *adelantados*, what were they but private entrepreneurs, to whom the Crown gave its blessing only after they had succeeded, just as King Alfonso had done in the case of the Cid, whose victories cost him neither effort nor money. In the epoch of the Napoleonic wars, once again, it was private initiative that rushed into the streets to save Spanish sovereignty, despite the abject submission of the monarchs.

This ardent impulse to private action, which colors the whole history of the Iberian Peninsula, explains why the first settlers of New Spain—and we see the same phenomenon in the other colonies—were aware of a difference between themselves and the newly arrived officials from the motherland, and already harbored within themselves the seeds of future independence. We still believe that, up to a certain point, the Spanish empire endured—despite the fact which has been called to our attention, that it was at war with the French, the Turks, the Germans, the Flemings, the Moors, and the English—not because of its system of administration, which was always inadequate, or its sea power, which was never really dominant, but because of the Spanish temperament, the character of a people whose nature it is to transcend institutions in an exuberance of personal energy. Their notion of religion, of the monarchy, and of liberty was that each was a miracle with scant empirical basis, but sustained by powerful ideals. There was no effective plan for colonization, but half Spain moved to America and began to live there according to its knowledge and understanding. This is the reason for our republics; this is the reason why the Spanish world exceeds by far the limits of the peninsular state. This is the profound meaning of the Iberian creation: a creation of the unknown soldier, whose name is plain Juan Spaniard.

COLUMBUS AND AMERIGO VESPUCCI

The life of Amerigo Vespucci is full of blanks: we know it only as a bare outline. He was born in Florence near the middle of the fifteenth century, and died in Seville in February, 1512. Son of a notary, he was wretched as a student of letters under the tutelage of an uncle, but brilliant in mathematics, cosmography, and commerce. He traveled in France. Back in his own country, and in the service of the Medici, he carried on business and trade with the Spanish outfitters of ships, and finally moved to Spain, where he had dealings with the Sevillian outfitters who freighted ships bound for the newly discovered lands. He made one or two trips to the Indies, it seems, and then, with the backing of Dom Manuel of Portugal, made his third and most famous voyage. The fourth, on which he tried to reach Asia by rounding the New World on the south, ended in failure. And then, perhaps feeling somewhat neglected by Dom Pedro, he looked to the Spanish monarchs for assistance; about this same time the ship-outfitter Cristóbal de Haro, the astronomer Ruy Falerro, and the illustrious Magellan were likewise looking to them and leaving Portugal. Columbus's affairs, at the moment, were getting nowhere. He approached Amerigo Vespucci and asked for his support at Court. There, in Toro, Vespucci succeeded in obtaining approval for his old plan for a trip around the New World by way of the southwest, and, with Vicente Yáñez Pinzón, he made a start on the tedious preparations. Once established in Seville, Vespucci married María Cerezo and became a naturalized Spaniard. He proceeded with his preparations but the Portugese claims, based on the Bull of Alexander VI, blocked his way and prevented him from carrying his project out. It is supposed that he made four more voyages, but two are unlikely and two absurd. Later he held the office, perhaps created especially for him, of master pilot in the Clearing House of Seville. And there he died, as supervisor of ocean traffic to the Indies, watching the ships come and go from his tower. Let us take a closer look at this second Italian concerned with the Discovery.

When Vespucci, in 1497, first crossed the ocean, Columbus had not yet entered the Gulf of Mexico, and nothing was known of America except the Antilles. The expedition that Vespucci accompanied sailed into the Gulf of Honduras, along the Yucatan Peninsula, and up the Mexican coast as far as Florida, or perhaps as far as Georgia. This did not prevent Juan Ponce de León from discovering Florida once again some years later, on his three-year search for the mythical Fountain of Youth. Two years later, Vespucci sailed as pilot with the expedition of Alonso de Ojeda. They reached Cape San Roque in Brazil, then sailed back up the coast as far as the Gulf of Venezuela. (It is generally agreed, nowadays, that the voyage of 1497 has been confused with that of 1499, and that the latter date is correct for the voyage to the Gulf of Venezuela.)

But Vespucci owes his fame to the third voyage, on which he wandered along the coast of Brazil, from San Roque southward, sailing through the Bay of Todos Santos, and perhaps touching upon the present site of Rio de Janeiro, as far as the mouth of the Rio Plata. There he veered in a southerly direction and came upon an unidentified region of the Antarctic, and thence turned back to Africa. This voyage definitely convinced Amerigo that the newly discovered lands could not be Asiatic, and it was then he conceived the idea of reaching Asia by rounding the new continent on the south. But he may have thought the South American land-mass ended at the mouths of the Plata. And his fourth voyage, indeed, was an attempt to find a southwest passage to that part of Asia vaguely known as the Moluccas. Others, similarly convinced that the new lands were not Asiatic, sought the passage to the Moluccas through a possible strait farther north. Columbus, had by now accepted the notion that the new lands were Asiatic, and was seeking the passage to the Gulf of the Ganges, which he imagined lay nearby. But not Vespucci. He was forming the plan that Magellan would carry out twenty years later. Unfortunately, he became separated from his captain, and, after exploring those Brazilian coasts already familiar to him from his previous voyage, he took on a cargo of precious woods and returned to Lisbon. As for the other voyages, they are not worth mentioning in this brief outline.

Every sort of argument has been brought into play to prove that one or another, at the very least, of Vespucci's voyages was imaginary. For instance, there is no testimony of the first voyage except the narrative by Vespucci himself, whose reliability was always in doubt because of the "jettatúra," the Italian curse of bad luck. And yet, there is no record in the Barcelona archives of the reception that the Catholic monarchs gave for the lucky Columbus. This, however, did take place, and nobody doubts it. Again, it has been objected that the narratives by Vespucci are mighty vague to be true, and that they omit such important matters as the peninsular shape of Yucatan and of Florida, which he seems not to have noticed. Some critics have remarked that he came in contact with such high civilizations as that of Yucatan without saying a word about them; that he fails to mention the Rio Grande or the Mississippi. But Marco Polo was in China, and has nothing to say about tea—a striking novelty—or about the Great Wall. On the other hand, those who defend the voyages point out that the first and most doubtful one is not related in full but in a condensation of a more extensive narrative which has been lost; that, in the general view, everything makes more sense if the hypothesis of the voyages is admitted; that there exists, besides, irrefragable evidence in the form of certain contemporary maps, bearing names and information that could come only from Vespucci, unless the probability of other voyages in addition to those already known is admitted; and, finally, that, while we are doubting, we may as well question the voyages of

Cabot, which have no more documentary basis, and yet are accepted as real and authentic.

If the lack of documentation can be used as negative proof, we can erase the better part of history. Time, moreover, has brought to light evidence that vouches for Vespucci's truthfulness.

Even though Columbus—whose earlier vision may have been different—died in the mistaken belief that he had discovered Asiatic shores, men of science suspected from the first that these countries were no part of the East Indies. They soon began to be called, in the papers of the Catholic monarchs, the West Indies, probably with the intention of rectifying an error or intimating a doubt. Columbus called them "New World," without giving the term any other than a rhetorical meaning. But the geographers of his day came to agree, little by little, that this was in truth a new world. The islands that had been discovered were certainly very close to Africa. This could not be Asia. Nor did the descriptions of nature and of society in the Antilles correspond to the descriptions of the Asiatic islands. (As for America farther north, it was still believed to be continuous with Asia.)

Vespucci was more complete cosmographer than Columbus. Vespucci studied his routes. His voyages along the American coast explored it far beyond the reach of previous discoverers, and—except for the Arctic and Antarctic regions and the tiny waist of Darien—made it possible to establish that America was a continent. And if he did not himself carry out the proof that Magellan would provide later, at least he prepared the way. Thus, his influence on the cartography of his day was much more important than that of Columbus.

More the professional man than Columbus, Vespucci was definitely less capable as the man of enterprise. He never did attain the leadership of an expedition, and he failed in his attempts to find a way around America on the south. But this modest man —one of the discreet, rather than a hero—had a fund of knowledge and a style in writing that are as fascinating as the voyages themselves (if indeed the narratives are by his hand). As for the fact that his name was given to the Continent, it was something he never lived to know. The rivalry between Columbus and

Vespucci is an error of perspective, a mirage on the part of posterity. It is known that the relations between the two men were most friendly, that the Admiral regarded the Master Pilot as devoted to him and "a most excellent man." Even Ferdinand Columbus seems to have had no slightest intimation of this error of perspective. Sensitive as he was about anything that might affect his father's fame, though the celebrated narratives were familiar to him, he never said a single word against Vespucci.

AMERICA'S BAPTISM

Even America's name, by whim of the mythological genius presiding over the Discovery, was a matter of accident.

At the beginning of the sixteenth century, in the imperceptible city of Saint-Dié, a mere dot hidden away in the Vosges, there was a tiny society of humanists who were also publishers. The founder of this Gymnasium, Gauthier (or Gutierre) Lud, had installed a printing press in the house of his nephew Nicholas. His proofreader, and most eminent collaborator, was Martin Waldseemüller, of Freiburg. Another member was the amiable poet Matthew Ringmann—"Philesius" to his friends. Another was John Basin, who had composed a manual on the art of letter-writing.

The notions of geography current in the century could not fail to reach Saint-Dié; and these students, before venturing to read the reports of the latest discoveries, turned their eyes first to Ptolemy, as a firm foundation. One day the Gymnasium decided to publish Ptolemy's *Introduction to Geography,* and supplement it with Vespucci's narratives of his four voyages: from Honduras to Florida or Georgia, along the Mexican coast; from San Roque to Venezuela, along the Brazilian coast; from San Roque to the Rio Plata, along the same coast, thence to some region of the Antarctic, thence veering to Africa; and the unsuccessful attempt to reach the Moluccas by rounding South America. Waldseemüller took charge of the printing and added some comments of his own, plus a preface dedicating the book to the Emperor Maximilian, signed with the pseudonym "Martinus Hylacomylus."

This volume, *Cosmographiae Introductio,* came off the press in 1507. It was an immediate bestseller, because it announced the news of a Terra Firma that was not the same as the one Columbus had announced to the world. Columbus, indeed, after reconnoitering the Antilles, had declared under oath that Cuba—his Island of Juana—was Terra Firma. He never did recognize as such the Terra Firma that he actually discovered.

Vespucci made his appearance in the book published by the scholars of Saint-Dié with the first reports on those regions that were attracting everyone's attention. They were paradisiacal countries where the dreams of the prophets seemed to come true. Bizarre customs, as described by Vespucci, gave Europe's tired mental habits hope for relief. The hammock was mentioned for the first time. The editors annotated some passages in Ptolemy with a view to bringing them to bear on the recent finds; and in two chapters they casually let fall such phrases as this: "We may fittingly call this new part of the Earth America today, in commemoration of the intrepid man who has visited it." The name, accordingly, should be applied, not to Columbus's Archipelago, but to the Terra Firma visited—or at least described and "interpreted"—by Vespucci.

The authors of the large Cambridge History suggest, perhaps because of the pompous language, that the naming was proposed halfway humorously. Another guess: without any serious intent. Waldseemüller himself, it seems, had forgotten all about it when a map of his was published six years later; and by that time everyone, except the one responsible, was calling the New World "America." At any rate, Vespucci died with no knowledge, not even an inkling, of the matter. We can say that, in general, the sixteenth century accepted the casual baptism by the scholars of Saint-Dié, and that the seventeenth century started the reaction against it, covering the name of Vespucci with obloquy, and that this attitude persisted in the centuries to follow (Bayle, Voltaire, and others are examples of it). The name America steadily caught on, just the same, thanks in good measure to the literary charm and lively interest of those narratives, and despite the sober objections of Miguel Servet and the indignant protests that begin with Fray Bartolomé de Las Casas. Men of letters have the right to take pride in this success, which owes so much to the persuasive power of art, and to the diffusive power of a tale well told, whether we regard them as authentic works by Vespucci, or as offhand compilations of works by others.

The labor has been roundly shared. Some dreamed of the New World; others found it; others explored and mapped it; others baptized it; others conquered it; others colonized it and incorporated it in European civilization; others made it independent. Still others, let us hope, will show it the way to felicity.

AMERICA'S DESTINY

We have discovered America. Now, what are we going to do with America? Here the spirit enters in. The crusade for America succeeds the mediaeval crusade. America's destiny, from this moment—despite history's errors and accidents—takes on, for humanity, the meaning of a field of trial, where justice can be made more equal, liberty more real, and happiness more complete and better distributed among men; a republic like those the sages dreamed of, a Utopia. To Europe's loftiest intellects, America's appearance was heralded by brilliant trumpet blasts. What a springtime of dreams! While America, like the sea nymph in the marine eclogue, was barely letting her head show, the book presses were turning out an almost vulgar spate of Utopian tales. The humanists revived the style of the political novel in Plato's manner and, their eyes fixed on the New World, busied themselves with schemes for a better day. Dogmatic ideas were cast aside in the face of strange new customs. The likelihood that other civilizations were closer to earth was pondered; and Peter Martyr's "naked philosopher," as full of natural virtue as the fruits of the soil are naturally full of juice, prepared the way for Rousseau's "noble savage." The vogue of American exoticism brought new literary spices. Quite different from the Oriental exoticism, which was purely aesthetic or picturesque, this American exoticism carried a moral and political purpose; its literature used the spectacle of America to convey an image set forth *a priori:* the Golden Age of Antiquity, the state of natural innocence—apparently without being conscious of the heresy implied in this argument. Who, among the masters of European thought, could escape this enchanting vision? Its effects are found in Erasmus, in Thomas More, in Rabelais, Montaigne, Tasso, Bacon, and Thomas Campanella. While Juan Ponce de León was deliriously seeking the fountain of eternal youth in Florida, the philosophers were asking the New World to furnish the stimulus for the political regeneration of all peoples. This is the true tradition of our continent, and we must not forget it.

The testimony of Montaigne is singularly expressive. The drama of the Discovery, as presented through his spirit, is accompanied by a bright music of ideas that moves us still. As Montaigne was well aware, the sheer contrast between the Old World and the New was what wakened him to that tolerance for all beliefs which Bacon and Shakespeare were to learn from him, that pardon, that compassion. During Montaigne's youth, America grew in importance, from day to day, and its increasing gravitation seems to have raised him steadily above the moral level of his time. He read with avidity every report by the chroniclers of the Indies; moreover, as an officer of Bordeaux, he could see and admire, as they arrived, the goods and products of those generous new lands. One of his servants who had lived for ten years in Brazil informed him about some native customs. Montaigne's interest was aroused; he translated the cannibals' songs and poems. Always ready for a paradox, he dared to wonder if, after all, our familiar civilization could not be a huge aberration; if the American man, "the Inca, splendidly naked, and the Mexican clothed in plumes"—as Góngora put it—might not be closer to the Creator; if customs did not have a merely relative basis. And he concludes by finding art and refinement among the Eden-like Tupí-Guaraní tribes. Sure enough, Montaigne admits to himself, those Indians are cannibals. But is it any worse to eat your fellow-men than to enslave and exploit them, as Europe does to nine-tenths of humanity? America tortures prisoners of war, but, Montaigne reflects, Europe permits worse tortures in the name of justice and of religion. And here we see sprouting, in the mind of a representative European, forecasts of the most advanced, even the most audacious views that the modern spirit holds. Dissatisfaction with European wickedness began to change the atmosphere. The effects of the contagion showed in Protestantism, in Puritanism, and especially in Quakerism, which finally took refuge in America. But meanwhile Catholicism, too, had experimented with social Utopias in the Mexican foundations of Vasco de Quiroga, in the first Brazilian missions, and in the Jesuit Empire of Paraguay.

What radiant promise the New World held forth to malcontents and reformers everywhere! While tradesmen were getting rich, the apostolic religions were carrying on their labor of redemption, and legions of dreamers moved toward hope. America, we can say without exaggeration, was desired and discovered (almost "invented") as a field of experiment for lofty ideas. America was created, discovered by those who suffered hunger in body or in soul, by those who required houses of gold to satisfy their craving for luxury, and by those who required freedom of conscience so as to spread and nurture the idea of God and the idea of good. Later, still a refuge for the persecuted, America became a home for the proscribed Huguenots and Puritans, a land where the accusing eye no longer hunts down the unregenerate sons of Cain.

Then came colonization by Europe. The process of gestation, for several centuries, weighed America down, and the ideal remained latent, asleep. If the seed was dropped at the moment of the Discovery, even when spiritual energy was channeled into viceregal administration, the seed still was warmed quietly beneath the soil. It was not dead, far from it. Little by little, as the republics won their freedom, the ideal was purified and made whole, and became universal. All through the nineteenth century the most ardent Utopians—spiritualists, socialists, communists—flocked to the New World as to a Promised Land, where happiness is for those who, under any of a myriad banners, aspire to it. And still the Continent welcomes hope and offers herself to Europe as a refuge for humanity.

Either this is the meaning of our history, or our history has no meaning. If this is not so, then it should be so, and all Americans know it. We may be turned from our path by accidents or foreign insults for a day, a year, a century, even, but the great ideal shall be saved. The trajectory of our America is as fixed as a star's. It began as an ideal and it is still an ideal.

Let us sum up. America, before she was ever discovered, was presaged in the dreams of poetry and in the glimmerings of science. The figure of the earth—not only the geographic but also the political figure—had to be completed. The king in the fable possessed but half a coin: he must get the other half in order to know his destiny. There were rumors, as in Plato's Atlantis, of a continent that sank into the waves, or, as in Seneca's Ultima Thule, a continent that lay beyond the ocean's horizon. America's absence was felt before her presence ever was. In the language of pre-Socratic philosophy, the world without America was a case of unbalanced elements, of disequilibrium, of hybris, of injustice. And for some time America fled before the prows of enchanted seafarers.

Once America had been discovered, the human mind, tirelessly seeking the triumph of the good society, set itself to imagining, on the ideal plane, Utopias and perfect republics, and set itself to building, on the practical plane, institutions with religious and political extensions that could never have fitted into the limits of Old Europe. The pretext, which called forth the miracle, had been a very humble thing: insurrection in the kitchens, deprived of Eastern spices by the fall of Constantinople to the Turk. The vehicle was a gross, material thing: economic exploitation of the colonies, lust for immediate riches. Above all this, however, the ideal sounded its march.

From then on, despite the vicissitudes and vacillations of history—for life never proceeds in a straight line—America has been the theater for every experiment in human happiness, every adventure in well-being. And today, in the face of the Old World's disasters, America is still worth a hope. Her very colonial origin, which has forced her to seek beyond herself the reasons for her own behavior and culture, has endowed her precociously with an international point of view, a grasp of the far-flung human panorama as a unified whole. Only American culture can ignore, forthrightly, racial and national barriers. Between the homogenous Latin sphere and the homogenous Anglo-Saxon sphere, democratic sympathies act as levelers and clear the way to *homonoia*. The American nations are not so foreign, one to another, as the nations of the other continents are. Three centuries of slow development; a century of hazardous experiment, disrupted by independence and reorganization; then, half a century of cohesion and collaboration. This, in broad outline, has been America's path.

Vision of Anáhuac

*Traveler, you have come to the most
transparent region of the air.*

I<small>N THE DAYS</small> of the discoveries there appeared books full of
marvelous reports and geographical adventures. History, faced
with new worlds to discover, departed from its narrow classic
course: political topics had to give way to treatises on peoples
and portrayals of civilizations. The historians of the sixteenth
century, while led by astonishment to exaggerate at times, painted
the character of the newly found lands for the eyes of Europe.
The tireless Giovanni Battista Ramusio issued his curious collection, *Delle Navigationi et Viaggi,* at Venice in 1550. This work
in three volumes, later printed separately, is rich with enchanting
illustrations. There can be no doubt of its usefulness: chroniclers
of the Indies in the seventeenth century (Solís, at least) found
letters of Cortés among the Italian translations in the book.

The illustrations, naïve and elegant, after the fashion of that
day, show the gradual conquest of exotic shores. Tiny ships
follow a line across the ocean. In the middle of it, a sea monster
writhes, coiled like a hunter's horn, and a fabulous nautical star,
in the corner, radiates fine spikes. Aeolus, from the bosom of a
stylized cloud, puffs his cheeks to indicate the direction of the
wind, always a matter of anxiety to the sons of Ulysses. There

are scenes of African life, under the inevitable grove of palms and beside the cone-shaped hut of straw with smoke rising from it. There are men and beasts of other climes, and panoramas in minute detail, and strange plants and islands out of dreams. And on the coasts of New France, groups of natives are hunting and fishing, dancing and building cities. An imagination like Stevenson's, capable of conjuring up *Treasure Island* from a child's atlas, could have spun, from Ramusio's pictures, a thousand and one delights for our cloudy days.

And then, there are illustrations that show the vegetation of Anáhuac. Let us give these our full attention: here is something new in the way of nature.

The ear of corn belonging to Ceres, the banana from paradise, the fruits swollen with strange honey . . . But, above all, the typical plants: The maguey (which, we are told, draws its juice from the rock), opening out from the ground to shoot its flowering plume high; the organ cactus, its parallel columns joined like the reeds of the Panpipe, useful for fencing boundaries; the disks of the prickly pear, imposed one upon the other in the manner of a candelabrum—an arrangement pleasing to the eye —and looking altogether like a schematic flower designed to emblazon a coat-of-arms. In the clean outlines of the engravings, with no color to blur their purity, fruit and leaf, stem and root are abstract patterns.

These plants bristling with thorns inform us that nature here is not, as in the south or along the coast, lush with sap and nourishing vapors. In the land of Anáhuac, fertility is to be found only near the lakes. But man, working like the beaver, has contrived, through the centuries, to drain their waters; he has felled the forest about his home, and the valley has been stripped to its naked hostile self. Barbed hooks, standing out sharply from the alkaline and inimical soil, raise their woody claws to fend off drought.

The drying up of the valley went on from 1449 to 1900. Three races worked at it, and we might say three civilizations—for there is little in common between the viceregal order and the prodigious political fiction that gave us, under the Díaz regime, thirty years of Augustan peace. Three types of monarchy, separated by parentheses of anarchy, afford an example of how the state's work grows and is corrected in the face of the same natural threat and the same earth that must be spaded up. From Netzalhualcoyotl to the second Luís de Velasco, and from him to Porfirio Díaz, the watchword, it seems, was "drain the land." Our century found us tossing the last shovelful, grubbing the last ditch.

There is quite a drama, complete with heroes and stage setting, in the draining of the lakes. Something of this is suggested by Ruiz de Alarcón, in his comedy, *El semejante a sí mismo*. In the presence of a numerous assembly, presided over by the viceroy and the archbishop, the sluices are opened, and the vast waters parade through the cuts. This is the setting. And the plot: the intrigues of the engineer Alonso Arias, the negative decisions of the self-satisfied Dutchman, Adrian Boot, until, finally, prison gates close behind Enrico Martín, who still holds his level high with a steady hand.

Like the specter of all the city's disasters, the brooding waters lie in wait, disturbing the dreams of its gracious and cruel people, washing bare its flower-covered stones, measuring its brave towers with baleful blue eye.

When the creators of the desert have finished their work, the social cataclysm thunders.

One question the traveler from the Americas cannot escape in Europe is: Are there many trees in America? They would be surprised if we were to tell them of an American Castile higher than the one in Spain, more harmonious, and certainly not so bleak (even though it is broken up by great mountains instead of hills), where the air has the brilliance of a mirror, and where it is always autumn. The Castilian plain inspires ascetic thoughts; the valley of Mexico, thoughts that are simple and sober. One is more tragic in feeling, the other richer in plastic form.

Nature, in our land, shows two contrasting sides.

There is the familiar virgin forest of America, which has been poetized so often, it is hardly worth describing. It has been an obligatory theme for the enthusiasm of Old World writers ever since it inspired Chateaubriand's wordy ebullitions. A furnace generating energies that are spent with lavish abandon, where intoxicating perfumes debauch the will, it is the image of life at its most intense and most chaotic: the cascades of verdure down the mountainside; the impenetrable tangles of creepers; the tented banana plants; the alluring shade of trees that entice you to sleep and then rob you of the power of thought; oppressive vegetation; insidious, voluptuous torpor; the hum of insects . . . And the screech of parrots, the thunder of waterfalls, the fierce eye of the wild beast, *le dard empoisonné du sauvage!* But, in the extravagance of sun-glare and languor, the poetry of hammock and fan, other southern countries surpass us by far.

What we have, in Anáhuac, is something better, more invigorating. Better, at least, for those who like to keep their minds unclouded and their wills alert. Our nature is to be seen at its best in the central plateau region. There, the spare and heraldic vegetation, the balanced composition of the landscape, the atmosphere so keenly clear that colors are drowned in it—a loss made up for by the general harmony of the design,—the transparent air, in which everything stands out in bold relief; and to sum it all up in the words of the modest, sensitive Fray Manuel de Navarrete:

> A resplendent light
> Which makes the face of heaven bright.

This was observed also by the great traveler who added with his name to the pride of New Spain; a man of classic and universal stature, like those men bred by the Renaissance, it was he who revived in his century the ancient mode of acquiring knowledge through travel and the habit of writing only from personal experience and meditation. In his *Political Essay*, the Baron von Humboldt noticed the strange refraction of the sun's rays on the mountainous mass of the central plateau, where the air is purified.

In that landscape, which is not without a certain aristocratic sterility, wherever the discerning eye may wander, the mind becomes aware of each line and revels in each undulation.

In that brilliant, cool and placid atmosphere, the unknown men who came into the valley feasted their broad spiritual gaze. Ecstatic before the cactus and the eagle and serpent—happy emblem of our countryside—they heard the voice of the prophetic bird, promising them refuge among the hospitable lakes. From huts of mud a city rose, peopled again and again by the incursions of mythological warriors who came from the Seven Caves, cradle of the seven tribes that dwell in our land. From the city an empire grew, and the roar of a giant civilization, like that of

Babylon or Egypt, still reverberated, though diminishing, in the woeful days of the feeble Moctezuma. And it was then that, in an hour we well may envy, Cortés and his men ("dust, sweat, and iron"), the snow-crusted volcanoes behind them now, stood wonderstruck on the rim of that circle of resonance and light, spaciously ringed about by mountains.

At their feet, in a shimmering crystal mirage, lay the painted city, all its streets emanating from the temple, radiating from the corners of the pyramid.

They could hear the wail of the flageolet, ululating through some dark and bloody rite, and, multiplied by echo, the beat of the savage drum.

II

"It looked like those enchanted houses
the book of Amadis describes . . .
I don't know how to describe it."
BERNAL DÍAZ DEL CASTILLO

Two lakes cover nearly the entire valley; one is salt water and the other sweet. Their waters mingle to the rhythms of the tide in the basin formed by the encircling mountain ranges and divided by a rugged spur that juts from them. The city, in the middle of the salt lake, is like an immense stone flower. It is attached to the land by four gates and three causeways as wide as two cavalry lances. At each of the four gates an official levies taxes on merchandise. The buildings are arranged in cubic masses; the stone is carved in designs and fretwork. The noblemen's homes have flower gardens on upper and lower terraces and rooftops where as many as thirty horsemen could tilt. The streets are sliced at intervals by canals. Bridges across the canals are of carved wooden beams, and wide enough for ten riders. Canoes made of tree trunks, filled with fruit, slip under the bridges. Along the canals people come and go, buying fresh water to drink. The red water jars pass from one pair of arms to another. Artisans and master workmen stroll about the public places, waiting for someone to hire them. Conversations are sometimes lively, but never noisy. The race has sensitive ears, and talk is often in a whisper. Soft hisses are heard, flowing vowels, consonants that tend to sound liquid. Their palaver is mellifluous music. Those x's, those tl's, those ch's, so formidable when we see them in writing, drip from the Indian's lips as sweetly as nectar of the maguey.

The people dress ornately, for they are in view of a great emperor. Cotton tunics, red, trimmed in gold, with raised embroidery, black and white, decorated with circles of feathers or with painted figures, come and go. The dark faces, calm and smiling, manifest the desire to please. Heavy rings dangle from ear and nose; about the throat hang necklaces of eight strands, colored stones, little bells, gold pendants. The plumes in their smooth black hair wave when they walk. Their muscular legs gleam with metal clasps, and they wear eyeshades of silver leaf trimmed in deerskin, yellow or white. Their flexible sandals make a soft slapping sound. Some wear boots of skins like mink, the white sole whipped on with gold thread. Their hands flutter many-colored fly whisks, or swing walking sticks carved like a snake, with mother-of-pearl eyes and teeth, knob of embossed leather, tassels of feathers. The skins, the stones and metals, the feathers and cottons, mingle their tints in a ceaseless iridescence and, reflecting their quality and refinement, give the people the delicate look of dolls.

There are three centers of life in the city, as there are in all cities worthy of the name: the house of the gods, the marketplace, and the emperor's palace. Each section and suburb has a temple, market, and palace on a smaller scale. This repetition of the municipal pattern sets a stamp of unity on the whole city.

The main temple is a triumph of stone. From the mountains of basalt and porphyry that rim the valley gigantic slabs have been rolled down. Few nations—writes Humboldt—have moved greater masses. From one corner of the pyramid's square base to another is a bow-shot's length. From the top the whole Chinese-like panorama can be seen. The temple supports forty towers, adorned with friezes; the interior is elaborate with images, secret chambers, woodwork carved in figures of men and monsters. The giant idols—says Cortés—are made with a mixture of all the seeds and vegetables that the Aztec uses for food. Beside them, the snakeskin drum whose ominous boom is heard two leagues away; beside them, conch shells, trumpets, huge knives. The temple is large enough to house a village of five hundred. In the wall surrounding it are carved slabs depicting knotted serpents, which will later serve as pedestals for the columns of the Cathedral. The priests live inside the enclosure, wear black robes; their hair is long and unkempt; they shun certain foods and keep strict fasts. The chosen daughters of noblemen are secluded nearby; they live like nuns and spend their days weaving feathers.

But the exhibits of skulls and the gruesome evidences of human sacrifice quickly repel the Christian soldier, who, on the other hand, spreads himself with zest on his description of the market place.

There can be seen in the market, he says, "everything that is to be found anywhere in the entire realm." And, he goes on to add, even other things as well, such as imported foods and silverwork. The main square, with covered walks all around it, is twice the size of the one in Salamanca. At least sixty thousand people—he would have us believe—pass through it daily. Each kind of merchandise is confined to a single street; no intermixing is allowed. Everything is sold by number and measure, not by weight. No cheating is tolerated: there are always secret agents mingling with the crowd, keeping a close watch for false measures, which they shatter. Ten or twelve judges in canopied chairs pass open and equitable judgment, without appeal, on the quarrels of the market place. Slaves also are brought to this great square for sale, each one tied to a long pole by a collar.

They sell there, says Cortés, jewels of gold and silver, of lead, of brass, of copper, of tin; bones, sea shells, and feathers; stones, carved and smooth; adobes, bricks, wood, carved and smooth. They sell also gold in grain and in powder, kept in feather quills, which, with the seeds in common use, serve as money. There are streets for wild game, where all the birds that flock in Mexico's varied climates can be found: partridge and quail, prairie chicken, wild duck, flycatchers, wood duck, doves, pigeons, and little birds tied to sticks of cane; owls and parrots, falcons, eagles, nightjars, hawks. They sell also the skins of birds of prey—feathers, head, beak, claws, and all. There are rabbits, hares, deer, muskrats, moles, opossum, and little dogs that are gelded to be eaten. There is the street of the herb venders, where they sell roots and herbs for healing; on these empiric remedies their medical knowledge was based. More than twelve hundred varieties were made known by the Indians to Dr. Francisco Hernández, physician to Philip II, and the Pliny of New Spain. To one side are apothecaries, selling salves, lotions, and medicinal syrups. There are barbershops where hair is cut and washed. There are houses where, for a price, one can eat and drink. Piles of wood, splinters of fat pine, charcoal and clay braziers. Mats for the bed, and finer ones to sit on or to cover floors. Vegetables in abundance, especially onion, leek, garlic, boragewort, nasturtium, sorrel, cardoon, and golden thistle. Capulins and plums are the fruits that sell best. Honey and beeswax, syrup of corn, smooth and sweet as that of cane, nectar of the maguey, good also for making candies and wines. Cortés, describing these syrups to the Emperor Charles V, tells him, with charming simplicity, they are "better than arrope," the Spanish preserves made with wine. The cotton fabrics displayed for curtains, ornamental cloths and scarves remind him of the street of the silk weavers in Granada. There are also blankets, ropes, sandals, made of fiber from the maguey. There are sheets of beaten bark, from which paper is made. There are tubes of cane filled with liquid amber, for perfume, or filled with tobacco. Colorings of all shades and hues. Oils of chia, compared by some to mustard and by others to fleawort, which make paint waterproof; the Indian still keeps the secret of the enamels that give luster to his gourds and wooden bowls. There are deerskins with and without fur, gray, white, fancily painted; skins of nutria, raccoon, wildcat, tanned and raw. Vases, jars, and pitchers of every shape and type, painted, glazed, of prime clay and quality. Corn in kernel and in bread, superior to that of the Caribbean islands or the Spanish Main. Fish, fresh and salt, raw and cooked. Chicken and duck eggs, tortillas made of other bird eggs.

The market place, with its movement and roar, astonished even those who have been in Constantinople and in Rome, says Bernal Díaz. It dazes the senses; it is like one of Brueghel's imaginings, where the realistic allegory sheds a spiritual warmth. The conqueror staggers, amazed, through the picturesque streets of the fair, and his memories retain the emotion of a strange, palpitating chaos; forms melt into one another; colors explode like fireworks, in jets and swirls; the appetite is stirred by piquant odors of spices and herbs. Rolling, overflowing from trays and baskets is a paradise of fruit: balls of color, transparent bubbles, lances in clusters, the scaly pineapple, green hearts of leaves.

Wooden tubs of sardines glisten with silver and saffron, fringes of fins, dainty brushes of tails. From a barrel emerges the beast-like head of a fish, bewhiskered and astounded. In the streets set aside for falconry sit birds with thirsty beak, blue and cherry wings half opened like a loosely held fan, claws earth-yellow, clenched like gnarled roots, the eye of a dead bird, round and hard. Farther along, heaps of beans and grains, black, red, yellow, and white, all oily and shiny. Then, the assorted venison: pro-truding from hills of loins and stacks of hoofs is a horn, a muzzle, a limp tongue. At the far end is the artificial garden of carpets and tapestries; there, too, the toys of metal or stone, queer, mon-strous, comprehensible only to this people that makes them and plays with them. The auctioneering merchants, the jewelers, the leathermakers, the potters, all grouped strictly according to trade, as in the processions of Alsloot. The breasts of the pottery seller blend with the dark hues of her wares. Her arms move about among things of clay as in their native element: they seem to be handles on the jugs, serpentine moldings on the dark red necks. A circlet of black and gold around the belly of the jars repeats the tones of the collar that clasps her throat. The widest pots seem to be seated, like the Indian woman, knees together, feet parallel. There is a gurgling sound of water oozing from pitchers of fragrant clay.

"The finest thing in the market place," declares Gómara, "is the work in gold and feathers, which copies anything and any color. The Indians are so skilled at this, they can make out of feathers a butterfly, an animal, a tree, a rose, flowers, grass, and rocks, so perfectly it seems alive or natural. It sometimes happens that they forget to eat all day, adding a feather, taking one away or fastening it down, studying it from every angle, in the sun, in the shade, through half-closed eyes, to see whether it looks best right side up or upside down or crosswise, from the front or from the back; in short, they do not let it out of their hands until it is perfect. Few peoples have so much patience, least of all those that are prone to anger, like our own.

"The craftsmen with the highest prestige and skill are the silversmiths. They offer for sale things elaborately worked with stone and molded by fire: an octagonal plate with alternating quarters of gold and silver, not soldered, but fused together; a pot with its handle made the way a bell clapper is made here, but loose; a fish with one scale of gold and the next of silver, no matter if it has a great many. They cast a parrot, whose tongue moves, and its head and wings. They mold a monkey that moves feet and head and holds in its paws a spindle which it appears to be spinning or an apple which it appears to be eating. The Spaniards are greatly impressed by these things: our silversmiths do not achieve such perfection. They furthermore know how to enamel, and to cut and set emeralds, and to drill pearls . . ."

Bernal Díaz was no authority in matters of art, but he reveals the enthusiasm that the Conquistadors felt for Indian craftsmanship. "There are three Indians in the city of Mexico," he writes, "who are called Marcos de Aquino and Juan de la Cruz, and El Crespillo, so skilled at wood-carving and painting, that if they had lived in the times of the ancient and famed Apelles, or Michelangelo or Berruguete, who are of our own times, they would have been ranked among them."

The emperor has copies made, in gold, silver, stone and feathers, of everything under the sun to be found in his realm. He appears in the old chronicles as a fabulous Midas whose throne was as resplendent as the sun. If there is any poetry in America, a poet has asserted, it is in the Great Moctezuma of the golden throne. His kingdom of gold, his palace of gold, his garments of gold, his flesh of gold . . . Did not he, himself, have to lift up his robes to convince Cortés that he was not made of gold? His dominions stretch beyond the limits of the known; to carry out his orders messengers speed to the four winds. When Cortés asked an astonished chieftain whether he was a vassal of Moctezuma's, he answered:

"And who is not his vassal?"

The lords of those distant lands live a part of the year at court and send their first-born sons to wait on Moctezuma. Each day as many as six hundred knights come to the palace; their servants and followers crowd two or three spacious patios and spill over and swarm in the adjacent streets. All day long a numerous retinue pullulates around the king, but without ever coming near his person. Food is served to all at one time, and the cellars and pantries are open to any who are hungry or thirsty. "Three or four hundred youths carried in the dishes, which were countless, for each time the emperor supped or dined they brought him every kind of food, meats and fish and fruit and vegetables, to be found in the entire land. And because the climate is chilly, they placed a little brazier with live coals underneath each dish and platter to keep it warm." The king sat on a leather cushion in the middle of an enormous room, which gradually filled with his courtiers, and, while he ate, he passed food from his dishes to five or six aged noblemen, who stood some distance from him. At the beginning and end of meals, serving-women handed him a wash-bowl, and neither the towels, the dishes, the bowls or the braziers used by him were ever used again. While he dined he was entertained with jests by his jugglers and hunchbacks, or listened to the music of Panpipes, flutes, conch shells, drums, and the like. A basin of incense burned by his side, and a wooden screen shielded him from view. The remains of his meals he gave to his jesters, and he rewarded them with jugs of chocolate. "From time to time," recalls Bernal Díaz, "they brought him, in cups of fine gold, a beverage made of that same chocolate, which they said strengthened his virility."

When the table was removed, and the people had gone, certain lords appeared, and later the jesters and acrobats. Sometimes the emperor smoked and rested; at other times a carpet was spread in the patio, and there was dancing to the beat of the hollow wooden drums. A shrill whistle signaled the drummers to start, and the dancers came in, costumed in rich shawls, fans, garlands of roses, and feathered headdresses that simulated heads of eagles, tigers, or alligators. Singing as they danced, all joined hands and began with gentle movements and in a low voice. Little by little they became more animated, and, to keep their spirits high, wine bearers moved in and out among the rows of dancers, pouring liquor into their jugs. Moctezuma "put on four different suits of clothing every day, all new, and never wore any garment twice. The noblemen who entered his presence always came in barefoot," and in an attitude of humility, with bowed heads, never looking him in the face. "Certain lords," adds Cortés, "reproved the Spaniards, saying that when they talked with me they were too free, and looked me in the face, which seemed forward and disrespectful." The noblemen took off their shoes, changed their rich robes for plain ones, and advanced with three bows: "Lord—My Lord—Great Lord." "When Moctezuma went into the city, which was seldom, those who went with him and those he met in the streets averted their faces from him, and the others prostrated themselves until he had passed," observes Cortés. A kind of lictor went before him, bearing three slender rods, one of which the emperor grasped on descending from his litter. It was a sight to remember when he came to meet Cortés, leaning on the arms of two lords, on foot, and down the middle of a broad street. His retinue, in two endless columns, followed, keeping close to the walls. Servants walked ahead of him, spreading carpets before his feet.

The emperor is fond of hunting. His falconers, it is said, never fail to bring down any bird they raise. His hunters, in a shouting crowd, surround the wild beast. But falconry is his favorite sport, the hunting of cranes, kites, crows. While some use snares for birds, Moctezuma shoots them with bow and blow-gun. The blow-guns, tube and dart, are a handspan long, of gold, adorned with figures of flowers and animals.

He has palaces and pleasure houses within and outside the city, and each is for a different pastime. The doors open onto streets and squares, with a vista of patios where fountains play, inlaid with marble like a chessboard; walls of marble and jasper, porphyry, basalt; walls striped red, transparent walls; roofs of cedar, pine, palm, cypress, all elaborately carved. The rooms are painted and carpeted, some with cotton fabrics, others with rabbitskin, others with feathers. The prayer room is decorated with silver and gold plaques, set with stones. All about the Babylonian gardens—where no edible fruit or vegetable is allowed to grow —there are galleries and porticoes where Moctezuma and his wives seek recreation, broad groves laid out in designs of plants and flowers, rabbit warrens, fish ponds, rocks, and hills where deer wander; ten pools of fresh and salt water for every variety of aquatic bird, each being supplied with its accustomed diet of fish or worms and insects or corn or special seeds. Three hundred men take care of them; still others tend the sick birds. Some clean the pools, others catch fish, others feed the birds. The duty of some is to delouse them, of others to gather the eggs, of others to set them when they are broody, of others to pluck them for their feathers. Birds of prey from hawks and falcons to the golden eagle, are kept in another section, in shelters provided with perches. There are also caged mountain lions, jaguars, wolves, foxes, snakes, wildcats, that make an infernal racket; three hundred more men are assigned to their care. And that nothing may be lacking in this museum of natural history, there are dwellings for families of albinos, dwarfs, hunchbacks, and other freaks.

There are granaries and counting houses, with shields over the doors bearing the figure of a rabbit, where treasurers, book-keepers, and revenue officers live; armories, with shields bearing two quivers, containing darts, slings, lances, war clubs, bucklers, helmets, greaves, wristlets, truncheons studded with blades of obsidian, rods for spears, rounded stones, and a sort of padded shield that unrolled, covers the warrior's whole body.

Four times the Anonymous Conquistador attempted to see each of Moctezuma's palaces: four times he gave up in weary despair. (The opinion today, it seems, is that the *Chronicle of the Anonymous Conquistador* was the invention of Alonso de Ulloa; that it was based on Cortés and adapted by Ramusio. The circumstance does not affect the authenticity of this description.)

III

The flower, mother of the smile.—EL NIGROMANTE

If nature's part in all aspects of Indian life was as important as the accounts of the Conquistadors tell us; if flowers were grown for the adornment of men and gods, and appear as a stylized motif in the plastic arts and picture writing, we can be sure to find nature and flowers in the poetry.

The epoch of Aztec history that saw the Conquistadors arrive in Mexico followed immediately on the rain of flowers that fell on men's heads at the close of the fourth sun cycle since creation. The earth made amends for previous austerity, and men waved the banners of joy. In the drawings of the Vatican Codex, a triangular figure decked with entwined plants represents the earth, to which the goddess of marital love descends on a swing of plants, while seeds burst in the heavens, raining down leaves and flowers.

The basic materials for a study of the artistic representation of the plant in America are to be found in the monuments of the culture that flourished in the valley of Mexico just before the Conquest. The picture writing offers the most varied and abundant examples: "flower" was the sign for one of the twenty days in the month; "flower" stood also for the noble and the precious, also for perfumes and wines. It springs from the blood of sacrifice and crowns the symbol for oratory. Garlands alternate with the tree, the maguey and corn in the signs for place names. The flower is drawn in schematic style, reduced to bare outline, either as seen in profile, or from the corolla's mouth. The tree, too, is represented by a conventional scheme: either a trunk that forks into three equal branches, topped with leaves, or two diverging trunks with symmetrical branches.

In the sculptures of stone or clay we find single flowers without leaves and exuberant fruit trees, sometimes as attributes of divinity, sometimes as personal adornment or decoration on utensils.

In the pottery from Cholula, the pots have a floral star on the bottom and calyxes interlaced all around, inside and out. The weavers' bowls have black flowers on a yellow ground; in many cases the flower is barely suggested by a few lines.

In the poetry, also, we find the flower, and nature, and the landscape of the valley.

We must deplore the loss of Mexico's native poetry, for it is irreparable. Scholars may occasionally find isolated fragments, or assess the relative fidelity of the Spanish translations made by the missionary friars. But none of this, no matter how important, can compensate for the loss of Indian poetry as social expression and as cultural contribution. Our knowledge of it does not go beyond vague conjectures and a few ingenuous narratives which the friars preserved, although doubtless understanding but dimly the poetic rites they describe. And our imagination retains only the fabulous early years of Netzahualcóyotl, the prince robbed of his kingdom, who lived for a time in the woods, on wild fruit, composing songs to solace his exile.

There remain, however, some curious specimens to prove what the role of nature must have been in that poetry; and these, in spite of probable adulteration, seem to be based on unmistakably genuine sources. There are, for instance, some old poems written in Nahuatl, of the kind the Indians sang on festive occasions, as noticed by Cabrera y Quintero in his *Escudo de Armas de Mexico*, (1746). Learned by heart, they transmitted from one generation to another the most detailed legends of the people's origins, as well as rules of conduct. Those who first came upon them passed them over in silence, assuming they were hymns composed in honor of the devil. The only versions that we have today could not be exact translations of the originals, for these were banned by the Church, although she tolerated, since she could not root out, the pleasant custom of reciting these poems at banquets and dances. In 1555 the provincial council ordered that they be submitted to Christian ministers for scrutiny, and three years later the Indians were again forbidden to sing them without the permission of their parish priests and vicars. As for the few that remain to us—nothing survives of those Fray Bernardino de Sahugún is said to have published, except the mention of them— we do not know who the author was, nor where they came from, nor when they were written, although they are believed to be genuine native works, and not, as some have thought, mere fabrications by the missionary friars. Scholars agree that they were collected by a friar for the purpose of submitting them to his superior; that, composed before the Conquest, they were put into writing shortly after the old tongue had been fitted out with the Spanish alphabet. Even though they come to us indirectly and altered, these songs have a range of sensual perception that was anything but characteristic of the missionary fathers, simple, apostolic souls, with more piety than imagination. On this dubious ground, however, we must be wary of surprises. May we trust that the striking similarity between some of these verses and familiar passages in the Song of Solomon is pure coincidence? We have been put on our guard by that collection of *Aztecas* in which Pesado paraphrases native poems, for these, critics tell us, reveal the influence of Horace on Netzahualcóyotl.

There is a boldness of image in the ancient Nahua songs, a certain incongruity that betrays a non-European train of thought. Brinton, who translated them into English and published them at Philadelphia in 1887, claims to find in one of them an allegorical intent. The poet asks, where shall I find inspiration? And, like Wordsworth, gives his own answer: in the great heart of nature. The whole world seems to him a sensitive garden. The song is called *Ninoyolnonotza:* profound meditation, melancholy delight, long, voluptuous fantasy in which the pleasures of the senses are transmuted into a search for the ideal. (The following translation of *Ninoyolnonotza* is by D. G. Brinton.)

NINOYOLNONOTZA

1. I am wondering where I may gather some pretty, sweet flowers. Whom shall I ask? Suppose that I ask the brilliant hummingbird, the emerald trembler; suppose that I ask the yellow butterfly; they will tell me, they know, where bloom the pretty, sweet flowers, whether I may gather them here in the laurel woods where dwell the tzinitzcan birds, or whether I may gather them in the flowery forests where the tlauquechol lives. There they may be plucked sparkling with dew, there they come forth in perfection. Perhaps there I shall see them if they have appeared; I shall place them in the folds of my garment, and with them I shall greet the children, I shall make glad the nobles.

2. Truly as I walk along I hear the rocks as it were replying to the sweet songs of the flowers; truly the glittering, chattering water answers, the bird-green fountain, there it sings, it dashes forth, it sings again; the mockingbird answers; perhaps the coyol bird answers, and many sweet singing birds scatter their voices around like music. They bless the earth, pouring out their sweet voices.

3. I said, I cried aloud, may I not cause you pain, ye beloved ones, who are seated to listen; may the brilliant hummingbirds come soon. Whom do we seek, O noble poet? I ask, I say: Where are the pretty, fragrant flowers with which I may make you glad, my noble compeers? Soon they will sing to me, "Here we will make thee to see, thou singer, truly wherewith thou shalt make glad the nobles, thy companions."

4. They led me within a valley to a fertile spot, a flowery spot, where the dew spread out in glittering splendor, where I saw various lovely fragrant flowers, lovely odorous flowers, clothed with the dew, scattered around in rainbow glory, there they said to me, "Pluck the flowers, whichever thou wishest, mayest thou the singer be glad, and give them to thy friends, to the nobles, that they may rejoice on the earth."

5. So I gathered in the folds of my garment the various fragrant flowers, delicate scented, delicious, and I said, may some of our people enter here, may very many of us be here; and I thought I should go forth to announce to our friends that here all of us should rejoice in the different lovely, odorous flowers,

and that we should cull the various sweet songs with which we might rejoice our friends here on earth, and the nobles in their grandeur and dignity.

6. So I the singer gathered all the flowers to place them upon the nobles, to clothe them and put them in their hands; and soon I lifted my voice in a worthy song glorifying the nobles before the face of Tloque-in-Nahuaque,* where there is no servitude.

Thus the poet, in search of the secret of nature, reaches the very rock-bottom of the valley. "I am in a bed of roses," he seems to tell us, "and I wrap my soul in the rainbow of the flowers." They sing all around him, and, truly, the rocks answer the songs of the blossoms. He wants to drown in pleasure, but there can be no pleasure that is not shared, so he goes out into the country, and calls to his people and to his noble friends and to all the children who pass by. And, as he goes, he weeps for joy. (The ancient race was solemn and lachrymose.) Thus the flower is the source of his tears and of his ecstasy.

It falls off appreciably at the end, and here, perhaps, the Spanish missionary put in his heavy touch.

We can imagine the singer, in a very simple form of drama, handing flowers to his table companions, suiting the gesture to the words. It must have been one of those little symbolic acts that we still find examples of in the ceremonies of the Church. Springing from the Dionysian rites, the rites of nature and of green growing things, they survive in the sacrifice of the Mass.

The wandering poet, searching for flowers and questioning the bird and the butterfly, recalls to the reader's mind the Shulamite in search of his beloved. The image of the flower is so frequent, it is like an obsession. Another song says, "Let us take, let us untwine the jewels. The blue flowers are woven upon the yellow, we can give them to the children. Let my soul be enveloped in flowers, let it be made drunk by them, for soon I must depart." To the poet, the flower seems to represent all the good things of earth. But these are worth nothing in comparison with the glories of the Divinity: "Even though the speeches be as jewels and precious ointments, there is no one who can speak suitably here of the giver of life." In another poem, part of the cycle concerning Quetzalcoatl (the most important cycle of that con-

---

* Tloque-in-Nahuaque: he comprised in his being the essence of all things, conserving and sustaining them.—Molina.

fused mythology, symbolizing the civilizer and prophet, and one
of the vaguely understood sun myths as well), there are descriptive strokes of wonderful conciseness that bring before our eyes
"the house made of light rays, the house of plumed serpents, the
house of turquoises." From that house, which, in the poet's words,
glitters like a mosaic of many colors, came the noblemen, who
"went out weeping over the water"—a phrase that throbs with
evocation of the city of the lakes. The poem is a kind of elegy
on the disappearance of the hero. It has to do with a mourning
rite, similar to that for Persephone or Adonis or Tammuz or any
of those that acquired popularity in Europe. But it differs from
the cults of the Mediterranean shores, for the hero's resurrection,
here, is far in the future; he may never rise again. Otherwise he
would have triumphed over the bloody, sinister god of the human
sacrifices and would have prevented the barbarous Aztecs from
imposing their domination; he would have changed Mexican history. The quetzal, the rainbow bird that was to announce the
return of this second Arthur, has migrated now to the regions
of the continental isthmus, perhaps foreboding a new destiny, "I
wept with the humiliation of the mountains; I was downcast with
the exaltation of the sands, because my lord had departed." The
hero proves himself a warrior: "My lord, in our battles, was
adorned with plumes." A few lines later we run into this disconcerting sequence: "After he had become drunk, the chieftain
wept; we rejoiced that we were in his room." ("The king hath
brought me into his chambers: we will be glad and rejoice in
thee."—The Song of Solomon.) The poet has fanciful thoughts:
"I come from Nonohualco," he says, "as though I were bringing
birds to the noblemen's house." And again he is haunted by the
flower: "I am desolate, as desolate as the last flower."

IV

But glorious it was to see, how the region
was filled with horses and chariots . . .
BUNYAN, *Pilgrim's Progress*

I am not among those who dream of an absurd perpetuation of
the Indian tradition, nor am I any too certain the Spanish one will
endure forever), we are united with yesterday's race—no need to

argue ties of blood—by the common struggle to tame the fierce rude nature that surrounds us, a struggle that is the very raw stuff of history. We are united also by the far deeper emotions aroused each day by the same natural objects. The impact of the same world on our sensibilities forges a common soul. But even if we do not accept the solidarity of shared effort, or the solidarity of shared emotion, we must agree, at any rate, that a feeling for history is an integral part of our modern life: without its glow our mountains and valleys would be like a theater without lights. The poet sees, when the moon glimmers on the snow of the volcanoes, Doña Marina's ghost silhouetted against the sky, pursued by the shade of the Archer of Stars. Or he dreams of the copper axe whose edge upholds the heavens. Or thinks he hears, in some lonely wild, the doleful weeping of the twins that the white-robed goddess bears on her back. Let us not scorn the evocation; let us not flout the legend. Even if the tradition is not our own, it is anyhow in our hands, only we can preserve it. We must not renounce, O Keats, a thing of beauty, which will create joy forever.

Mexico's Three Kingdoms

Vulgar sapience counsels us not to put faith in appearances. No advice could be more appallingly mistaken, for we are surrounded all our lives by nothing but appearances, like those prisoners in Plato's cavern who were permitted to contemplate only the shadows of things. To take appearances on faith, and then delve into them, interrogate them, is the only way to acquire any kind of knowledge, whether religious, philosophical, ethical, artistic, or scientific.

The sense's first impressions are sacred. It makes no difference if they must be corrected or interpreted later. The precious gift of eyes, the divine present of light—without it we could not enjoy the "twenty atmospheres" which Velázquez has condensed, according to Gautier, in the ambient air of his "Ladies in Waiting" (*Las Meninas*), nor could we figure out the form of the universe, whether in Newton's old image, or in Einstein's modern one.

Geometry was worked out with eyes, and even the air itself is architecture, to quote Santayana's happy phrase. When the sage's vision, in the ancient fable, was torn from him, the obligation was felt to grant him clairvoyance, in exchange, as with Tiresias, as with Homer. For only prophecy or poetry could compensate us for such loss. That terrible holiness of Quevedo's stoic, who exclaimed: "I have lost my eyes! I have lost the means of losing my soul!" might just as well be turned about to its reverse: "I have lost the means of losing my soul!"

The admirable photographs by George Hoyningen-Huene (*México Eterno* [Mexico, D. F., Atlante, 1946], *Mexican Heritage*, [New York, J. J. Augustin, 1946]) through their mute eloquence—not being decked out in titles or verbiage, which always distract to some extent from the immediate simplicity of the impression—perform the noblest of all charitable works: they give back sight to the blind. No sociological study, and no amount of economic statistics can rival, as a way to understand a people, the profound intuition of an album of photographs, this gallery of ecstatic appearances, in which Mexico shows her face with all its expressions: sensibility, pathos, melancholy, gaiety.

Thus, the supreme master of Spanish criticism, Menéndez Pelayo, when he made his first approach to the spectacle of our poetry, was well advised to seek the sources of its originality above all in those very effects of the landscape on the mind. And thus Jaime Torres Bodet has said that the phenomenon of the landscape is confused and submerged in the greater phenomenon of the national literature. And when we say literature we mean the whole expression of a people's soul. Without light—without light and shadow—it would not be possible for us to understand certain paradoxical effects of "aloofness" (as Coleridge called it), which our poetry lapses into at times, as when, for instance, our Modernist bards shut their eyes, momentarily, to the living sights of our America. For, in rejecting their environment, they leave us a transparency through which we can make out the environment they wish to reject.

The entire complex scheme of forces that we call human geography, without which no one can comprehend history, is nothing more than the reaction, the answer of our will, to the natural and planetary system that envelops us; whether we think of Egypt in Herodotus's way, as a gift of the Nile, or whether we think of it in Toynbee's way, as an answer to the "challenge" of the Nile. The Colombian historian Germán Arciniegas offers this apt observations:

"If some curious spirit should set about reconstructing the history of light in America, he would decorate the stage where the Conquest, colonization, the wars of emancipation, and the nineteenth century had their showing with landscapes totally unfamiliar to us." It is impossible to understand a people's conduct without making this effort to recreate the atmosphere.

For this work of the future, Hoyningen-Huene's Mexican album has inestimable value. And we ourselves tried to take a few steps in that direction, describing the table land of Anáhuac as "the most transparent region of the air."

We still feel the presence of the ancient gods, concealed, or rather incorporated in the features of the natural physiognomy. Tree and stone seem to breathe a kind of religious air. Those remote ancestors who trod Mexican soil centuries ago assumed, as all peoples have, that the gods circulated in the "vital space" surrounding them. This is the sort of hieroglyphic interpretation that man's conscious mind has always tried to apply to the things of this world among which he must shape his behavior.

Those ancestors, during a long process of intellectualization, put aside the merely imitative or mimetic modes of representing things, for which their technical equipment (fortunately!) was as yet inadequate. And so they developed, step by step, artistic forms compact with symbols, which can be read almost as clearly as writing.

The contortions and monumental flights of the Mexican archaeological record—art forms born of religious impulses—which are like a written lesson on the universe, represent precisely an effort to delve into ambient appearances and to understand them in a human way.

This human way is still very different from our own. But it is a human way that we can understand, perhaps, only if we try to compare the same text the ancient Mexican used to study (the landscape and the atmosphere: a section in this album) with the lesson he learned from that text—with the archaeological record.

Without this interplay of actions and reactions, there would be no meaning to art. The world asks and man answers. And the answer, in all truth, turns out to be, as often as not, still another query, for our enigma is far from being solved. Thus, the enigma expressed in art answers the enigma of the atmosphere, of natural forms, of the surroundings that envelop us, caress us, torment us. Thus, Mexico's archaeological record answers—in its terrible and transcendental manner—the queries of the Mexican landscape.

Upon this first terrace, the terrace of the Indian, the waters of another civilization, carried with them by the Spanish conquistadors, would later fall. This too was powered by a religious purpose. Then the Christian Cross was raised upon the ruins of the Aztec temple. And, little by little, on that same natural soil, changes were seen in that other, human, soil that we call civilization.

Landscape, Mexican archaeology and Mexican colonial art make up the present album, being the three indispensable phases of the process. The modern period is cosmopolitan and bland; which is to say: neutral and without national character. For this reason it is passed over. And a noble antipathy for the facile and alluring tricks that draw the tourist trade has inspired the creator of this album with the brave esthetic resolve to eliminate the human figure. Man is present only as a pair of eyes; that is, in contemplation. Tiny god who has finished his work, he is permitted only to look at what he has done. And it is well done! Our history need have no regrets.

Apart from, and in addition to, their materialistic motives and their greed for discovering paradises built of gold (the Emperor Moctezuma went so far as to strip himself naked in order to convince the conquistador Cortés that he was not made of gold), the Spaniards who overran our soil were soldiers of Christ, knights of a new crusade. This means their first churches were also fortresses and barracks. On the hilts of their swords they carried a cross.

No doubt, they were inspired, besides, with an eagerness to see miracles. This same eagerness, this same insatiable curiosity impelled Alexander, over his warriors' protests, beyond the known limits of the world, after there was no longer the slightest strategic or political excuse for the headlong dash. But the comparison should not be overdrawn, for Spanish realism has always managed to hold fairly well in check the impulses of Spanish fantasy, the madwoman in the home.

Finally, we cannot deny the Utopian inspiration through all the deeds that brought about the discovery and conquest of America, the hope that a better field could be found in which to try out experiments for human happiness.

During the colonial period, Mexico gradually acquired her historic physiognomy. The tides of conquest became calm, and with the intermingling of bloods a ceremonious and courteous people was born, whose very provincial tone tended to point up and emphasize somewhat the vanity of aristocratic rank. This is revealed in the works of the comedy writer Ruiz de Alarcón, the first universal voice to come out of Mexico. It is revealed also in the extremes of the "Mexican baroque" style in architecture, where Spanish haughtiness is mingled with the convulsive inspirations of indigenous art.

And then . . . the land tends to become uniform. There is mutual influence between nations. Independence moves toward interdependence (which is not the same as dependence). The iron bonds of economics tie the nations together. And let us hope that, from all this, an aurora of human fraternity will rise, above boundaries, above dictatorships, above the old imperialisms.

Mexico in a Nutshell

HE AZTECS, a race of warriors, ruled by terror over a number of heterogeneous tribes, and the only ones that escaped their empire were the very distant or the very brave, like the proud republic of Tlaxcala, whose sons preferred to cook their food without salt rather than to have dealings with the tyrants of Anáhuac. The Aztecs lived on the remains of ancient and mysterious civilizations, whose traditions they themselves were beginning to misinterpret, emptying them little by little of their moral content.

The peoples of America, isolated from the rest of the world, had gone through an evolution different from that of Europe, and it placed them in a relative position of marked inferiority. They were ignorant of true metallurgy and unacquainted with the use of beasts of burden, for which they substituted slaves. They made international agreements to wage war against each other every so often, in order to have human sacrifices for their gods. Their system of hieroglyphic writing had no provision for setting down the forms of language; consequently their literature could be preserved only through oral tradition. They were not able, either physically or morally, to withstand the encounter with the European. Their collision with the men who came from Europe, dressed in iron, armed with powder and ball and cannon, mounted on horseback and sustained by Christ, was the clash of the earthen pitcher with the cauldron. The pitcher may have been very fine and very handsome, but it was sooner broken.

The artistic feeling of those people still amazes us. And their descendants, vanquished a thousand times by regimes that seemed designed to crush them, still show proof of wondrous manual aptitudes and rare esthetic gifts. But the cannibal, similarly, can trace on his body tattooed patterns that no civilized person could match. Civilization is a moral and political product. The gift for art, like the gift for life, is a different—a free and sacred—order of life.

Cortés, a great political mind, played a game of intrigues and stratagems; he took advantage of the respect that the Indian always showed to anyone who claimed the title of ambassador, and introduced himself as such so that all doors would be open to him. He also took advantage of the superstition that made him appear as emissary of the Sons of the Sun (the real lords of the Mexican soil, who, according to the oracles, would one day return to take back their own), and, protected by the lucky apparition of the comet, he triumphed without a struggle over the frightened mind of the Emperor Moctezuma, who behaved toward him like King Latinus in the *Aeneid* on the arrival of Aeneas, the man of destiny. Moreover, he took advantage of the panic that the mere presence of Spanish troops aroused in the minds of the Indians: he passed the horses off as gods and the riders as centaurs. Finally, Cortés mobilized against the formidable central power the hatreds of a hundred outcast tribes. And so, under the inspiration of Cortés, the Indian themselves accomplished—for his benefit—the conquest of the Aztec Empire.

Without the fundamental weakness of those civilizations, already in ruin, and without this set of circumstances so singularly placed at the service of the enterprise, it would have been unattainable. Not only morally, but numerically unattainable. Could a few hundred men and a few dozen horses have achieved so huge a victory? Of course not. As in the *Iliad*, all the forces of heaven and earth took part in the conflict.

II

The penguins that St. Mael baptized were changed into men by dictate of heaven: it was imperative to sustain the honor of the sacrament. The Church, nevertheless, takes pity on those who are often regarded by the ignorant as beasts or as spawn of the devil. The Indian was at least admitted to the lowest category, as an elementary human being, and was allowed to receive the benefits of catechism and of baptism. The conquistador, violent and greedy, was inclined to reward himself with lands and with souls for his services to the Crown. The Church had the responsibility of keeping him, so far as possible, within bounds; she thereby rescued the flocks of Indians and continued to guide them toward the true Christian life. The rural populace, accustomed to living in a kind of agricultural communism, found itself divided up by the conquistador into partitions and *encomiendas*, or protectorates. The partition of the soil was the actual fact; the protectorate of souls was a bloody euphemism. And the Church rushed to protect the Indian populace: she took care of its lands, and gathered the terror-stricken families into the atrium.

From taking such good care of lands and families, she ended by owning them, converting the whole countryside into a garden of the Church, and raising herself up as one more lord, who challenged the power of the lay lords and countervailed the authority of the viceroys themselves. As early as the time of Philip IV, the councils of ministers talked of seizing the lands of New Spain from the dead ecclesiastical hand, for the stagnation of so much wealth was becoming a menace. The colony was being eaten up by the cyst within its breast. Charles III busied himself with the Family Pact and the conflicts of Europe: thus, although he expelled the Jesuits, he did not attack the real economic problem. More and more the feeling grew that the birth of a state within a state was not to be tolerated.

During three centuries the races mixed as they pleased, and the colony was governed and maintained through a miracle of respect for the monarchic idea and through a religious submission to the categories of the state. For the motherland scarcely wielded any but a spiritual force in America, being, as it was, unequipped with a naval force that would measure up to the vastness of its conquests, and even unequipped with American armies, which were improvised only at the last moment. Meanwhile a new nation—with the Indians underneath, the Spaniards on top, and the arrogant and domineering creoles and the astute and subtle mestizos in the middle—was quietly being evolved.

III

When the Napoleonic Wars overwhelmed the motherland, the liberal leaders in New Spain, inspired by the philosophy of the French Revolution, made a rush for independence. If they had not succeeded in starting a revolution, as Justo Sierra says, it is conceivable that the Church would have provoked one, seeing herself threatened now by the Crown. In any case, it is highly significant that there should appear, among the insurgent leaders, so many village priests.

On the night of September 15, 1810, the curate of the town of Dolores, Miguel Hidalgo y Costilla, called his parishioners together by sound of bell, and threw himself into the struggle against Spanish rule and for national independence. From those rioting country folk, from that mob of men swept on by a divine fever, poorly armed with picks and axes—each one as best he could, with the instruments at hand—there swelled the first great army of independence: an army which would turn out to be formidable, and which would come to a stop only on the Cerro de las Cruces, held back by heaven only knows what mysterious compulsions or considerations, just when it was on the verge of descending on Mexico City, where the triumph seems to have been assured. The majesty of history does not always see fit to find easy solutions for great conflicts.

On the night of September 15, to honor the humble and unforgettable deed, the president of the Republic assembles the people on the military plaza in Mexico City, facing the National Palace, that somber and majestic edifice vested with grief and history; he tolls the same bell with which the curate Hidalgo sounded the alarm in the nation's heart, and repeats the ritual shout: "Viva Mexico, free and independent!" The scenes of rejoicing and festivity which then take place, amidst the answering roar of "Viva!" and the thousands of lights, are among the most picturesque details of Mexican popular life, and have enticed our novelists who write of customs and folkways. The breath of yesteryear's panegyrics seems to float over the handsome city.

This uprising of the people of Dolores, this deed—one among so many and such various deeds—has come to be regarded, for a number of historical reasons, as the symbol of independence—

which was not consummated, however, until ten years later, in 1821, by Colonel Agustín de Iturbide. While the liberals of Mexico dwell on the historic image of the curate Hidalgo, popular leader, true Father of the Nation, the conservatives dwell on the undeniable importance of the work of Iturbide—a creole aristocrat—as consummator of national independence. But Iturbide tarnished the luster of his image when he later committed the error of setting himself up as emperor of Mexico. His was an ephemeral empire, without historical justification or the slightest basis in popular sentiment. Hidalgo still keeps the high prestige of martyrdom for a noble cause—which was harder to fight for in his day than in Iturbide's.

Naturally, many forces worked together in the beginnings of emancipation. The social phenomena were very complex, and as for the wars and revolutions—those accelerated drives—it may be said that they tended to purify their motives and their purposes as they progressed. The people take up arms by instinct, and often do not discover what was their real desire or the principal cause of their anxieties and unhappiness until some years later. This is also true of the Mexican Revolution of 1910, which appeared in the beginning to be motivated by the sole purpose of getting rid of a man who had clung to power for longer than the laws of nature seemed to condone. But once the emotions of the people were violently stirred, all their grave and secret problems, which poured a vague, persistent pain throughout the body of the nation, began to make themselves known: social justice and a dignified status for labor, equitable distribution of the land, the incorporation of the Indian race into civilized life, and the joys of tranquility, a bulwark against those powerful peoples who have menaced us at times in their blind natural expansion; problems, in short, requiring intensive education—that is what they all reduce to. Similarly, in our struggle for independence, there is evident, in the background, a clear impulse toward political autonomy; but this impulse, when it first appeared, was clouded by many other accessory impulses, which commenced by collaborating with it and then vanished one by one.

The Mexican clergy also, a rural, humble clergy, weary of forever having to support the loftier personages of the Spanish ecclesiastical aristocracy, saw its advantage in the movement for independence. Hidalgo himself came from this social class.

And, as we have said, the Church looked with dismay upon the temptation to abolish mortmain which had infiltrated the councils of the Spanish Crown.

Finally, the conservatives and absolutists in Mexico dreamed of offering Ferdinand VII a Mexican throne, independent of Spain and unsoiled by a constitution . . . for let us remember that Spanish liberalism, by this date, had already trimmed the absolute powers of Ferdinand VII, by means of the Constitution of Cádiz. Taking only this one aspect of the question (which has its equivalent in the other republics), the paradoxists have tried to show that the independence of Spanish America was the work of monarchists. This amounts to saying that fire—a thing so grand and tremendous as fire—is an element that has for its purpose the lighting of cigarettes.

IV

Knowledge does not permit us to lie. True independence does not exist so long as there remains an aftermath of bitterness and dispute. True independence is capable of friendship, of gratitude, of understanding, of forgetting. Spain was great, so great that she conjured up against herself all the ambitious, and thus the Black Legend was born. The Spanish regime shared all the philosophical errors of its time. Other empires made the same mistakes or worse, but—being less great—were less conspicuous to the world. A Greek proverb says: "The slip of a giant's foot makes a racetrack for a dwarf." The Spanish performance was so mighty, the Spanish hand weighed so heavily on the earth, that its slightest move seemed gigantic—especially in the eyes of other peoples, less fortunate then, who contented themselves with pursuing the treasure-laden Spanish galleons, or scrabbling under the imperial table for leavings from the Spanish feast.

The valid fault to be found with the Spanish regime is that Spain never had forces with which to hold down her colonial dominions; that she never learned how to exploit her colonies intelligently, with the sound calculation of the tradesman, but instead went fantastically mad over them, gave herself to them, threw herself at them, all the while being visibly drained of her blood. And instead of building those huge commercial factories which the empires of the nineteenth century spawned, she produced nations capable of living their own lives as soon as they were ready to break away from the maternal tutelage. A fortunate fault, to be sure!

No Mexican can recall without gratitude the felicitous daring represented by the Laws of the Indies, in which we men of today seek inspiration for the campaign to defend the Indian, to safeguard the *ejidos* (the communal lands) of the towns, even to affirm the state's right of eminent domain in the national subsoil —always inalienable according to the Latin principles which have given to the world its juridical conscience.

No, we can say that independence, in its deepest and truest moral and political meaning, was aimed as much against the state as against the past. But sometimes I think it was rather against the past. Thus, the independence of the Americas and the inauguration of the republic in Spain are two parallel steps in the same historic evolution. Both were governed and justified by the same philosophy. The Hispano-American was cursing the Spaniard before he ever won independence. In his feeling of manly brotherhood—which now is no longer afraid of a natural interdependence—and of friendship and equality, we recognize the man who has succeeded in achieving real independence.

V

Would you wean a baby with absinthe? Well, we must realize that the American republics were born under the inspiration of a political philosophy that is actually a political philosophy for adults only. From an absolute and theocratic monarchy, a central and unified government, which had always been the political system in Mexico, before and after the Conquest, we passed to the Rights of Man and the federal constitution. We lived for a long time as though caught by the tail and dragged about by the chariot of an ideal we could not attain. The people had not been educated to take part in democratic representation, our whole pattern of customs was alien to the workings of the federal machine, the Indian was unprepared to rub shoulders with the white landlord possessing haciendas and owning influence in the city . . .

The ideas imported from France and from the United States were converted into high hopes by everyone, even by those who failed to understand them. Fray Servando Teresa de Mier (in his celebrated *Discourse on the Prophecies*) foresaw all the ills that would overtake the nation if she persisted in following ways that were foreign to her character and history. The Jacobin idea, liberal and individualist, predominated. And in the duel of advanced federalists and reactionary centralists, the chieftains marched in and took over, each of them determined to be president against the will of the rest. At the very outset, Iturbide determined to be something more: to be emperor. Great confusion. A great lesson.

At any rate, the duel of liberals and conservatives gradually created a rhythm of ebb and flow that more and more resembled a heartbeat, a coherent circulation, the respiration of a being already an individual, already in the process of organized growth. The face of a new people was being carved with knives. The scars were giving it character. And in this way the first half of the century was spent.

VI

The conservatives having been defeated for the moment, and the Church being threatened with the abolition of mortmain (a conflict that had become traditional), certain dupes committed the unpardonable error of asking Napoleon III to found an empire in Mexico. They wanted to put an end, once and for all, to the liberal Utopias, put a stop to anarchy, and delegate the national authority to more experienced hands, thereby saving it (as they thought) from the nascent peril which the proximity of a powerful people to the north implied. Then something happened that was like the bursting of an internal abscess. The malignant humors entered the blood stream and caused damage everywhere. But sometimes the body succeeded in eliminating them.

The conservatives, because of the recent bitterness, were relegated to the category of outcasts, as accomplices of the invader, even though some of them were patriots and men of good faith. And the liberals, crushed at the outset, rose up again with the genuine and solid backing of the nation, with a clear sense of their responsibilities and of the only possible road ahead. In the mind of the savior of the republic, Benito Juárez, or rather in his will, the metal of the fatherland, until then mixed and formless, was heated and definitively molded: it came out already forged into a sword.

Juárez has been criticized. The criticism concerns a number of small details which do not matter here. Criticism matters to us when it refers to his performance as a whole, to his general orientation. This criticism follows, in some cases, the path that we call passion. In others, the path that we shall call, rather than any form of action, inertia. The result of these criticisms is the obfuscation of the historical evidence. The effect on political culture is demoralization. I will clarify these concepts: passion, inertia, evidence, demoralization.

Passion: I do not, if you please, make use of the word with aggressive intent. Passion offers an integration of human stimuli which, if it is not consciously misdirected, deserves a measure of respect. To those who disagree with the political philosophy of Juárez I concede the same right to probe that I claim for myself. But I consider that these impassioned ones, although they are entirely on their home ground when they deplore the direction which Juárez gave to national progress, are out of bounds when they forget that the road opened by Juárez was, under the circumstances, the only possible road to the salvation of Mexico. I am not discussing principles, I am pointing out facts.

Inertia: The evidence that I have just pointed out, is also denied by those who suffer from inertia of the mind. One of the most acute and dissimulating forms of mental laziness is blind incomprehension, acquired from a crawling posture, in the face of the obvious: an inability to be objective; the impotence of the logical processes when confronted by facts which should be recognized as facts. The hankering to be original—ludicrous at bottom—is responsible, in the second place, for this vagary of the mind. Adverse critics, I have said, may *deplore*, but they may not *deny* the evidence. I say now, some of them through inertia, and others through an obsession with paradox, are not content with refusing to acknowledge facts: they actually want history to be interpreted—in the manner of Pérez Galdós' comic character—not as it happened but as they judge it should have happened. Why, of course! If only there had been no duel between liberals and conservatives! If only there had been no foreign intervention!

The concept of evidence has already been clarified by implication. That of demoralization can be reduced to the prospect of the sinister effect on civic education which would result from scanting the debt we owe to the austere pilot who saved the country.

VII

Let us recapitulate. Nobody has seen a river when it is being formed, when it has not yet made its channel, nor chosen a definite course. But history is much swifter than geography, and we can more clearly discern, in the perspective of memory, the first steps of a nation, her gropings toward autonomy, and then the crises and convulsions on the way to the achievement of civic liberties.

The forerunners thought only of offering the king of Spain a throne cleansed of all the "dangerous innovations" that French liberalism brought to Spain. This new entity, the Spanish people, which made its appearance in the *Cortes* of Cádiz, what could it have to do with New Spain? Nothing. New Spain belonged to the monarch. If Old Spain placed restrictions on the monarch, then Mexico must be torn away from the European motherland and offered, in all the purity of absolute dominion, to the Man of Divine Right.

An instant later, everything had changed: Hidalgo, the Father of his Country, had conceived the ideal of a free nation, and he fought and died for this cause. Morelos fought and died in open battle for social reform. And when Iturbide, in another instant, parted the Gordian knot with a sword, the nation was still so naive that she allowed herself to get caught in the trap of an ambitious imperial dream.

But a secret instinct—like that deep gravity which governs the flow of water and brings together the branches of tributaries so as to swell the river more and more and draw out its course over the surface of the land—a secret instinct spoke in the ear of the people, and told them that once the great obstacle had been overcome, once the great sacrifice had been made, the best thing was a bold choice of the ultimate and most promising design for national liberties. And that was the republic. And the republic began to grow, between the ebb-and-flow, the push-and-pull of those who, on one side, insisted on tradition, and those who, on the other, insisted on hope. This ebb-and-flow was inevitable, even indispensable; it performed the function of circulation and augured the viability of the new political being. But in the beginning it was often agitated, involved in reactions and asphyxias, disturbing the embryo and, on occasion, killing it.

In time, this ebb-and-flow of liberals and conservatives was on the verge of destroying the young republic. Then Juárez appeared, as that last providential point in which the vitality and the consciousness of a being in danger could take refuge. The nation was reduced to the proportions of the coach in which Juárez traveled. Juárez-Aeneas: Juárez, the man who emerged from the flames. Second Father of his Country, but now with the experience acquired through the vicissitudes of half a century. In that immense "first draft and new account" which it was his task to complete, he traced the course by which the river must flow, and opened a clear-cut new era in our history. For the first time a conscience made a clean sweep of deeds piled up by chance, and began to build it all anew with a sure plan, with an unswervable purpose. Now it was no longer blind nature: it was human intelligence. From the forehead of Benito Juárez leaped the winged image of the republic.

And when this daughter of the spirit, with the passing years and with badly distributed prosperity—"nineteenth-century materialism"—put on flesh, became middle class, and threatened to lose the sound economy of body and soul because of her unhygienic life, then she had to be subjected to an ascetic and gymnastic life, to a revolution as to a surgical operation; her figure had to be restored, and she had to be placed—as we say today—on a regime: on a new regime, which was concerned with a great deal more than diet.

The reform laws and the Constitution of 1857 remain like written tracks of that final duel between liberals and conservatives. The laws and the constitution, even so, were small things in comparison with what still had to be done, but, while they were often evaded, sometimes by subterfuge, sometimes by force, they made possible a halt on the road. This halt, affording the body which had suffered from shock a recuperative sleep, was the Porfirian peace.

Nevertheless, Hidalgo, Morelos, Juárez still had much work ahead of them. They had not yet taken off their campaign boots.

VIII

The scene changes. Peace, stability and soothing balm for the wounds of the Fatherland. Great respect for legal appearances. A spirit of conciliation toward former adversaries, the conservatives and other representatives of the so-called interests. Concentration of power in a single will, overbearing, but moved by unimpeachable love for the country, and so independent and secular that it did not need to stoop to gross extremes.

Dogmas of the epoch: first, peace above all. Peace as an end in itself, with all that this presumes and implies, including the suppression of certain salutary twitches of unrest. Deception and force? Governments have always used them. Blood? Much more has flowed before and since. Second, "little politics and much administration"; which is to say: put off as long as possible certain questions of theory, and attend to the immediate and the practical, but only in a very restricted sphere. The people were born to be governed by financiers, by the *"científicos,"* as they called themselves. Third, the notion of the foreigner as idea-force: let the foreigner hold a good opinion of us; let him feel at ease among us and give us his credit and his confidence, since the international customs-mark of approval comes from outside. This was the theory that the nation should be molded to fit her surroundings, and should not be born of her own entrails. It was the centripetal and not the centrifugal theory of the nation. It was the concept of evolutionary positivism, which prevailed in the public schools of those days: the being is a product of environment; consequently, the proof that the being possesses the proper conditions for life will consist in the world's gliding and turning around the country as if caressing it. (That awakening of nationalism at the hour of the revolution, nationalism which even took on aggressive airs at moments, can be explained, in part, as a reaction against this mythology of the foreigner). And foreign capital came in, the credit of the country rose, and, more or less linked with the oligarchy of the *científicos*, the privileged classes throughout the country—which were the ones that made their voice heard, for the people groaned in undertones, or failed to realize that their ills were caused by any political error—commenced to enjoy an era of blessings. And all forgot that the first need of a people is political education. The great leader, hero of a hundred battles, and now too a hero of peace, took care of everyone's conscience. Even the moral problems of individuals came to depend on his decisions. Parents brought their rakehell sons before him, so that he would throw a scare into them, or, if need be, send them into the campaign against the Yaqui Indians. The states of the republic came to be the convolutions of his brain. "Tlaxcala hurts me," he would say, and lift his hand to some region of his head. And one hour later, as though brought by the wind, the governor of Tlaxcala stood trembling before him.

How could there be, in the face of this example—grand and impressive as any, for Porfirio Díaz was a man of gigantic stature —how could there be anyone among us who could still preach doctrines based on the abandonment of political education? In spite of one man's good will, capital had come to be exclusively a force for exploitation, an irresponsible and mechanical energy, an economy of gain and not of service. It despoiled the nation and degraded labor.

Time did its work; the sleeper began to stir. The suspended body awoke from its torpor, and the soul—vacillating till then— began to clamor for its rights. The leader, grown old, had done his work, and was not wise enough to retire at the right time: at a time of multiplying problems which were really not his responsibility, which did not pertain to his view of the world. The old man believed he was surrounded by men like himself, but he was alone. A crystal wall shut him off from everything, an abyss of time, a mathematical dimension impossible to outmaneuver. One small indiscreet word, a vague suggestion about the fitness of allowing the people to have a try at holding elections on their own, and the spirit of the country awoke and began to work itself up like a storm. That giant who had known how to bring off triumphantly so many difficult tasks had not been able to create a successor for himself, blocked, no doubt, by the inevitable bad habits of dictatorship. Getting rid of the old president seemed to be the main problem of the revolution, and it turned out to be the easiest. As when an attempt is made to prevent an earthquake by sticking a dagger into the soil, or to prevent the eruption of a volcano by carrying out buckets of lava, the notion of writing off a revolution as finished just because a president had resigned turned out to be a chimera.

Actions followed upon reactions. The old army did not intend to give up without a fight. The oligarchy of interests and all the affiliated and conservative forces fought back. And after the coup of Victoriano Huerta, the real revolution, which had marched from north to south with Madero, amid acclamations and flags, returned over the same road with Carranza, but now amid blood and fire.

The revolution triumphed in an instant. The energies of Carranza were spent subduing his own chieftains and haphazard generals. For this reason, obliged to govern as a combatant and without constitutional forms, he was not able to recognize the moment when his successor was chosen by actual popularity. He tried to crush him, as though he were one rebel more, and fell, a victim of self-deception.

The revolution spent ten years searching for itself. Much of this was the discomfort of a man who wakes after a long sleep. Everything had to be set right, and it was natural to fall back on all the remedies known to political hope: formulas for workers' socialism and formulas for agrarian socialism, systems of corporations and of syndicates, prescriptions for the redistribution of the land, and for the regulation of labor in the cities. And above all, schools, schools. A grand crusade for learning electrified the spirit of the people. Nothing to equal it has ever been seen in the Americas. It will be Mexico's highest honor in history.

From 1920 on, the march of national reconstruction is more clearly glimpsed; governments followed one another in an orderly manner. Uprisings failed; each time they were headed by figures of smaller stature. The applications of the new constitutional principles gave rise to gropings, conflicts, misunderstandings, inside the country and out, which little by little quieted down and began to approximate the orderly pace of law.

That effervescence, that enthusiasm for what is national which we have mentioned, had for its reason, besides the one cited, the effective blockade to which Mexico was subjected during the European War because she had failed to define her position, occupied as she was in the solution of her own internal conflicts. Then everything had to be drawn from within her own substance

—and the country took stock of her genuinely great potentialities. It was like discovering again the patrimony once forgotten, like digging out of the earth the hidden gold of the Aztecs—that evocative legend! So we had all this in our house, and we never knew it? But—would we really have known how to use our treasure to the best advantage?

Some have pitied us with a certain condescension.

Now the hour has arrived for us to pity them in turn.

Pity those who have not had the courage to discover themselves, for they have not yet undergone the agony of this enlightenment!

But let them know that—as Scripture says—only those may be saved who are prepared to risk everything.

The Early Chroniclers

THE VERY knowledge of America's existence rejuvenated Europe's mind and will. In the realm of action, there was great stir among reformers, colonizers, and adventurers, and soon hope soared among the discontented, stifling in social stagnation, the Pilgrims, the Huguenots. In the realm of thought, not only were novel and exotic sauces added to the literary fare, but the impetus given to the humanist tradition of the perfect republic brought forth flights of political speculation and Utopian fancy. In the field of historiography,* where the affairs of governments and doings of the ruling class had always received preferential treatment, the spectacle of societies that were utterly fantastic forced an abrupt awakening: there was a new curiosity about people in the mass, and the subsoil known as ethnography was brought to the surface.

Then some of the pioneer historians of America emerged from among the travelers and writers of Europe, either because they had taken part in the discoveries—like Columbus, Amerigo Vespucci, the chaplain Juan Díaz of the Grijalva expedition—or through sheer enthusiasm, like Ramusio, the compiler. At times there was outright catering to the popular vogue: Pietro Bembo went to the length of inserting a chapter about the New World

---

* I call "historiography" all literature about history, to distinguish it from "history," the sequence of human events.

in his book on Venice. But the clear-sighted Jesuit, Acosta, an independent historian who lived in Lima and spent some time in Mexico, draws some apt comparisons between Mexico and Peru in his *Historia Natural y moral de las Indias,* certain generalizations that reveal a maturity of approach. The Spanish Conquest, when it came under the discipline of law, was recognized with the appointment of an officer *ad hoc:* the Chronicler of the Indies, whose position, like that of the Chronicler of Aragon, was created by the Emperor Charles V. The Chronicler of the Indies was an individual until the middle of the eighteenth century, when his duties were taken over by the Royal Academy of History. There were, besides, non-official writers like Gómara, attached to the staffs of military chiefs and to the households of governors in the capacity of chaplains or the like. Some of these historians, who have been overlooked, strangely enough, by Menéndez y Pelayo, are perfect exemplars of the classical and artistic type described in his famous academic discourse on history as a fine art.

All this belongs, of course, to the history of history, and not to the panorama of Mexican literature, which has not yet begun to unfold. These authors are given a place in our handbooks, in recognition of their priority as pioneers, and because of the gratitude that we owe them as a nation, but they are previous to Mexican literature in point of time and alien to it in substance.

Pietro Martire d'Anghiera, known as Peter Martyr, wrote the first treatises on ethnography and collected unique information. Somewhat slovenly in composition, he was always a fetching narrator—"the first literary inebriation with the tropics"—and he hardly allowed his obligations as official apologist for the Conquest to trammel him. His skepticism in the face of tall tales is relaxed only when they come to him disguised in the semblance of the classical myths: reminiscences of Hesiod's Golden Age, the isle of the Amazon women, a gallery of heroines in the manner of Livy, Columbus in the attitude of a Roman statue.

Gonzalo Fernández de Oviedo came no nearer to Mexico than Hispaniola or Santo Domingo. His pages on Mexico—though consulted in manuscript, perhaps, by Gómara and others—did not circulate in his time, but remained unpublished (some say because Las Casas objected to them) until scholars dug them up in the middle of the nineteenth century. An untidy writer with

relatively scant background—"he scarcely knew Latin when he heard it"—uncritical of his sources but a shrewd observer, he is esteemed by foreigners as a milestone in the evolution of historiography; his countrymen belittle him as endowed with more patience than intelligence.

Francisco López de Gómara, on the other hand, was a bred-in-the-bone man of letters, a master of economy in style, even if affected simplicity makes him monotonous in spots. He was one of the first artists to take a hand in building the oversized monument to Cortés, whose distention destroys the balance of the group as a whole.

This attempt to deify Cortés provoked resentment, and we have two outstanding examples of this reaction, one wild and one tame, if we may characterize them so summarily. Bernal Díaz del Castillo, on his own initiative and at his own risk, speaks for the ranks who (as Solís puts it) were born to be silent and to obey. And the humanist Francisco Cervantes de Salazar takes, naturally, a very different tone; he was named Chronicler of Mexico one day by the conquistadors and their offspring and the other gentry making up the cabildo of the City of Mexico, for they were eager to see the true facts and corrections that they had to offer him set down in his noble prose.

Don Antonio de Herrera was the first who tried to paint, in the antique rhetorical style, a world that eluded it in all directions; and while the fact that he wrote a complete history of the Indies argues a facility that explains his success, he betrays his presumption by amassing digressions and discourses and piling up a confusion of incoherent annals.

Don Antonio de Solís was the last who tried to conform to the difficult humanist model, piecing out his cloth with laces snatched from the purple of the Greco-Latin Clio, and accommodating, with elegant style, his interpretation of the Conquest to an ecclesiastic and providential conception of history.

II

Our literature is homemade. Its earliest genres are the chronicle and the missionary theater—plays intended to help spread the Gospel.

The Indian's culture, gorgeous and fragile as a flower, was con-

tent with living for the day, yet the Spaniard's, like all those of Europe, was interested in its own self-preservation. There was, then, a careful accumulation of materials, from the very beginning, and this was the start of our historiography.

The primitive chronicle does not have the same purpose as beautiful letters, but it inaugurates them and accompanies them up to a certain point. It was the work of conquistadors anxious to perpetuate their fame; of missionaries, in close touch with the Indian soul, who disdained notoriety and in many instances did not take the trouble to publish their books, and to them we owe what little remains to us of the ancient native poetry; and, finally, the work also of the first Indian writers, who incorporated in the new civilization, and torn between two languages, could not resign themselves to seeing the memory of their elders die out. Soon there would appear in this company an *encomendero* or so, who, in the leisure afforded by newly acquired land and wealth, would write for pastime; and there were academic scholars, assigned to gather information.

III

The first accounts of the Conquest were written by the conquistadors themselves. In this they followed a tradition, of which there are many examples among the Spanish warriors of the sixteenth century, who set down their exploits boldly, just as the Great Captain does in his chronicles, with the theoretical aim of showing the superiority of the Imperial troops.

Hernán Cortés, in his five famous letters, written to the Emperor Charles V between 1519 and 1526, tells the complete story from the landing at Cozumel through the Honduras expedition. He could as easily have sent in dry military reports. But, carried away by his gift for expression, he bequeathed to us a thrilling narrative, which, for all his air of objectivity and cool appraisal, pulses with life.

The Conqueror's writings, always straightforward, are as impetuous as speech and racy with household sayings and even proverbs—notwithstanding the fact that these reports were addressed to the Imperial Person—and manifest the feeling for lively style that Vossler praises in his study of Benvenuto Cellini. With all due respect for one of the critics we most highly vener-

ate, we find nothing in the manner of his writing that could be called "nervous" or "hasty." On the contrary, what surprises us is his tone of calm reflection in the midst of military alarms.

Gracián, an extremely precious writer for whom the enigma is a principle of esthetics—"to bring everything out into the open is neither useful nor in good taste"—declares that Cortés, the magnificent soldier, would never have been able to rise above mediocrity if he had chosen a literary career. Which is to pass judgment on something that never happened. Quevedo asserts that whosoever called letters and arms "sister arts" was mistaken, "for no two things can be more different than doing and saying." There are many instances that confute him, and the most impressive are those where the author's saying is about something he has done extremely well. The books are full of such instances.

There can be no denying that the one-time student at Salamanca, who knew his Latin, was somewhat of a poet. According to Díaz del Castillo, he expressed himself in very good rhetoric when he spoke to educated men; he adorned his harangues to his soldiers with heroics out of novels, and, quite apart from his natural gift for charming and convincing, showed a pronounced literary bent. And he returned to letters in his old age, founding in his own home the first academy in Spain on the Italian model. Here was a meeting-place for men in search of stimulating talk, such men of eminence in the humanities and in government as the liberal Cardinal Poggio, the learned Dominican Pastorelo, Archbishop of Callar, and numerous others.

With marveling eye and pen Cortés paints the life and customs of the country, its cities, its arts, its ceremonies; and he describes them all with an enthusiasm and a minute attention to detail that he never accords to his own deeds. For, evincing a rare equipoise between temperament and calculation, he makes few apologies and accepts soberly and imperturbably both his failures and his successes. A traveler who seeks to understand, he is not dismayed by what is strange. A narrator without peer, his descriptions are singularly vivid, and he makes no attempt to conceal the awe that Indian culture inspires in him. His letters add up to a hymn to "Mexican magnificence," which is evoked as powerfully in his rude rushing prose as in the poem that the elegant Bernardo de Balbuena will intone with artistic finish and sonorous measured syllables—and no doubt the letters are more sincere. The emo-

tions aroused by the wonders of the New World are more genuine in the chroniclers than in the poets, Humboldt avers.

But the moment an event or a circumstance, no matter how unforeseen, happens to fit in with his plans and offers him some advantage, though it may seem to us one of the most fantastic flukes in history—as when Moctezuma, a-tremble with mystic terror and undone by the anguish of presentiment, tells him of those fatal prophecies about Quetzalcoatl which have morally disarmed him, a second King Latinus before Aeneas, emissary of fate—Cortés turns instantly cold and moves his chess piece coldly. He shuts his eyes, steels his soul, and thinks only of his advantage. The realm of action, or rather the realm of the brain, banishes contemplation. The spirit of conquest assumes full sway.

This change of heart corresponds to the two phases of the campaign. The first phase was all persuasion and enchantment; it closed with the arrival at Tenochtitlán, and throughout it Cortés dreamed of a possible agreement, of capturing his prey by means of cunning alone. In the embrace that Cortés was tightening about his conquest, while there was blood, there was also love, and he himself felt conquered. For this reason it has been said that, if the letters are our commentary on the Gauls, even though Cortés can not match Caesar in purity of professional style, he surpasses him in enthusiasm and in sympathy. He even had visions of a political chimera so tremendous, that he could shunt aside his primary impulse of greed. Later, and despite the reverses that he suffered, this chimera—perhaps it was revealed in the privacy of the family group with a frankness that could inspire ambitions of autonomy in the minds of his sons—took on the shape of a vast Chinese-Mexican sphere which would have moved history's point of gravity, and which the inauguration of the viceroyalty prevented with one stroke.

When the second phase opened, however, and Tenochtitlán leaped up like a wild beast aroused, and Cortés had to seek refuge in disastrous flight; when he realized that all was not going so well; when the bandage dropped from his eyes, and he was heard to moan, on the summit of the temple in Tacuba, where, contemplating the city, he passed through the most painful crisis of his life; then he reacted like the lover who, blind and callous to any will other than his own, suddenly finds himself deceived.

And then the purely military phase began. The soldier replaced the seducer. He no longer saw any way out except through violence.

Thus, the course of the Conquest was determined by the conflict in his mind. This conflict explains the cruelties and imprudences that more than once ripped the net so astutely woven during his climb toward the central plateau of Mexico. It explains the impatience with which he strove to obliterate the abyss of religion which separated him from the goal he desired, as though one man's decision could accomplish in one minute the labor that wore out the missionaries. Cortés blames everything on Narváez's ill-advised expedition, on Velásquez's jealous anxiety to maintain his feeble semblance of authority. For the quarrels between Spaniard and Spaniard tarnished the prestige that the Sons of the Sun had begun to enjoy among those frightened witnesses of their conduct. But the fault lies deeper: it is in Cortés's contempt for the national and religious sentiment of the Indians, in his refusal, at times, to recognize that basic instinct which is called by a thousand names and which rouses us to struggle against any attempt at domination by an alien will.

IV

One of Cortés's men, Bernal Díaz del Castillo, combatant in more than a hundred battles, and finally city magistrate in Santiago de Guatemala—where he proudly gathered, one day, the fruits of the seven orange trees that he brought as seeds from Spain, just as the aged Andrés de Vega would share with his comrades the first three asparagus that grew in the plains of Cuzco— this old soldier would write, regardless of consequences, in the rough language of the encampment and with a view to old grievances, that "True History of the Conquest of New Spain," whose very title is a reply to the challenge of Gómara, a work overwhelming in its sincerity and in its charm without artifice, "a triumph of memory . . . the long yarn of an old man who threads his memories together beside the fire," which gives off, as we read it, the pungent and salubrious odors of the wild thicket. Nor does the humanist influence that pervaded all that epoch fail to show. Even though Bernal Díaz "is no Latin, nor

does he know anything about art," he makes very apt allusions to the figures and deeds of antiquity, with a frequency that would put a modern scholar to shame.

Díaz del Castillo faces reality with the common sense of Juan Spaniard and with the bluntness of the people, wary of the miracle mongering, the interventions of the Apostle James, known as Santiago, and the legendary exaggerations which had already begun to distort the image of the knights of flesh and blood. The brave, in his pages, are not ashamed to tremble, as they do in life. Glory is not made of marble and monumental gold, but of weariness and suffering, "of sun and dust," as the romantic put it. Here is the voice of the soldier, never in the least disrespectful to the chief, always loyally obeyed, but exasperated by those who fail to understand the true fraternity of danger, where each man gives the other his hand—a voice that demands a place in the triumphal march, and asks for a sprig of the garland that is granted only to the captains. The protest of Bernal Díaz is directed at the two adulators of the one and only hero, at Gómara and Solís. "A beautiful example of soldierly indignation," observes Fitzmaurice-Kelly. The chronicler remembers each and every one of his comrades-at-arms, and would be able to describe them, even though they number nearly five hundred; and for each one he demands, at the least, the tribute of gratitude.

Although Díaz del Castillo is not to be ranked behind Cortés as a father of history and as a narrator of events, perhaps he makes his heart more warmly felt. There are cries of pathos in him and applause for performances, for those of his comrades and those of his enemies as well. It is absurd that historians confined to their libraries should try to convict him of vainglory, when the exploits he boasts of still amaze the world. His astonishment at the sights that he meets in our country causes him to drop the reins and lose his footing in the stirrups. He never tires of expressing his wonder at so much, and such extraordinary, excellence. In his high-flown judgment as a lay expert, he compares the Indian craftsmen (Marcos de Aquino, Juan de la Cruz, El Crespillo!) to Michelangelo and Berruguete. And nowhere is he more ecstatic than when he views the Aztec Troy for the first time: a work of enchantment, he says, and a dream from the "Book of Amadis."

V

The one that Clavigero has called "the Anonymous Conquistador" is included in this group simply because he was a soldier. Perhaps the thirty-odd pages that are the extent of his narrative were intended as an introduction to a history of the Conquest. What little we have, a succinct and entertaining description of the Mexican antiquities on the arrival of the Spaniards—sketches of the countryside and the cities, of the life, religion, and customs of the inhabitants—is broken off abruptly, "leaving us with the honey on our lips." An amiable and wise tourist, that Anonymous Conquistador.

VI

In their reconstruction of that past which goes as far back as the ancient kingdoms, their culture, archaeology, and ethnography, the missionaries and the Indian historians have done eminent service. Very valuable indeed, but beyond our scope, is the work of the gentle and courageous Motolinía, of the indefatigable and meticulous Sahagún, of the honorable and incorruptible Mendieta, of the rude and honest Durán. There are important works by the Tlaxcaltecan Muñoz Camargo, and by Alvarado Tezozómoc, grandson on the maternal side of Moctezuma II, and by Fernando de Alva Ixtlilxóchitl, a rather labyrinthine historian.

VII

There is, finally, a cycle that is polemic rather than historical, represented by Fray Bartolomé de Las Casas and his partisans and opponents. The unforgettable Bishop of Chiapas commenced at the first opportunity, and sustained to the end of his long life, a furious defense of the perfectly rational nature of the Indian, inveighing against the errors of the ruling class, the feudal origin of its crimes, the partitions of land and the *encomiendas*, the inhumanity of the conquistadors; he indited a monument of Christian charity, of which it can certainly be said that "the style is the

man." The controversy over the natural rights of the Indian has not yet ceased in our day, and we even see negative contentions boiling up in the least-expected places. It all brings to mind the discussion between angels and saints when the blind St. Mael, as the story goes, administered the rites of baptism to the penguins. If the story has aroused laughter, the reality has brought tears.

VIII

Among the texts in Nahuatl gathered by Sahagún in order to redact his *Historia*, which appeared in two successive Spanish versions—a labor that consumed more than thirty years—there is a jewel, a fine example of the things that can be found in some of the books by missionaries. It is the story of the Conquest as told by several old and princely Indians and put together by the scholars at Tlaltelolco under the direction of Sahagún. It is possible that these literate Indians may have composed for themselves a cultivated language differing from the old Nahuatl; we do not know.

At any rate, the recent translation of this work has unique value; it permits us to compare the same deeds as seen from two different points of view: from the conquistador's, and from that of the conquered. We find in it, besides, a transition from the heroic approach to the historical approach, which is a remarkable phenomenon. The narrative is still imbued with poetic dew; the style and the imagery throb with mythological fervor. Moctezuma sees, in a mirror, that a strange prophetic bird wears in its topknot the image of the approaching conquistadors, in the shape of canes hoisted on deer, since the horse was unknown in America.

There is barely space to mention the Chronicle of Chac-Xulub-Chen, by the Maya chieftain Ah Nakuk Pech, another important document on the history of the Conquest as seen by one of the conquered. The narrative adheres to canons of composition which Augustín Yáñez sums up thus: "We are surprised, at the very beginning, at the markedly Oriental rhythm, a most subtle internal rhythm, which Nakuk-Pech employs. Oriental, too, is the architecture of the chronicle, divided into paragraphs in the manner of verses, in which themes and epithets are reiterated in cadence. Oriental is the plastic style, full of imagery, thesis

and antithesis, of a solemn and religious beauty: 'As for me, my name is called Nakuk-Pech, and not because water ever entered my head. There came one night the day of war . . .' "

We can add to these the defiant recitals of their own deeds with which the fierce Itzas, on the shores of the Petén, tried to intimidate the conquistadors; also a history of Michoacan, concerning the tribulations of some Tarascan chieftains on Lake Pátzcuaro, written for the Viceroy Mendoza by an Indian poet who still could not distinguish fact from fable.

Fray Servando
Teresa de Mier

I: HIS LIFE

The "Memoirs" of Fray Servando Teresa de Mier, of the convent of Santo Domingo in the City of Mexico, and deputy to the First Constituent Congress of the Republic, are a mélange of comic and tragic episodes related in a sprightly and colorful style.

Fray Servando was born in Monterrey, capital of the Mexican state of Nuevo Leon, in the latter years of Spanish rule. His life can be divided into three periods; the second one corresponds to a protracted exile from his native land.

During the first period, or until 1795, Fray Servando was a forerunner of Independence. He was representative of his time and his profession, for the idea of revolution had percolated by then through all the social classes and was being fomented by the Mexican clergy.

But one day we see Fray Servando ejected from his country, banished. He roams the Spanish peninsula and France and England, fleeing always from the persecution of the Church. And what is his crime? A daring sermon, a theological spoof, which

only too transparently revealed the underlying separatist thought. During the second period of his life, then, Fray Servando wandered as an exile in Europe: first in Spain, where he was treated to a sampling of ecclesiastical jails; next in France, where he became a friend of Simón Rodríguez, who was Bolívar's mentor; he said Mass in a chapel, and taught Spanish to little boys by means of a translation he claims to have made of Chateaubriand's *Atala*. Later he went to Rome, where the pope granted his petition to be released from his vows. He returned to Spain and was again jailed. He escaped to Portugal, where he lived three years under the protection of the Spanish consul. When the Spanish war for independence broke out, Mier appeared as field chaplain of the Valencia volunteers. The French captured him at Belchite. He escaped, as usual, and was awarded honors by the Council of Seville. He went to London to work for the cause of Mexican independence. It was the day of Blanco White. Mier lived among the Spanish exiles; in spite of his somewhat bewildering volatility, he was a man of weight and persuasive gifts; it was he who convinced Mina the Younger he should undertake the celebrated armed expedition to fight for the independence of Mexico.

Fray Servando opened the third period of his life by returning to his homeland at Javier Mina's side. He shared the sufferings of the expedition, and, once again made prisoner, escaped from the guards who were sending him back to Spain, went into hiding in Havana, fled to the United States. He returned to Mexico while the new regime was still unsettled, and again he was persecuted and jailed. Soon we see him as deputy to the First Congress. Then Iturbide made himself emperor, and Mier—who had opposed him openly—landed in prison once more, only to be rescued by the republican revolution. From then on, Fray Servando was installed at the side of the first president, Guadalupe Victoria, in the National Palace. There he died, after personally inviting his friends, on the eve of his death, to be present at his last communion.

II: HIS CHARACTER

He is remembered in the political history of Mexico for his "discourse of the prophecies," in which he predicted many of the ills that have subsequently come to pass, one after the other. Mier was a moderate liberal, an adherent of the central republican government.

But what endears him most to his countrymen is the rollicking fantasy that filled his life. He lived more than sixty years and spent half of them as a fugitive from persecution. He seems, indeed, to have suffered persecution almost gladly. A kind of prophetic gaiety sustained him in his misfortunes, and he lost no occasion to fight for his ideals.

He was light and fragile as a bird, and apparently possessed that gift of "levitation" with which the saints are endowed, according to the students of miracles. At dodging, at vanishing, he was artful as a specter. A hundred times he was captured, and a hundred times got away. So amazing are his adventures, they resemble fiction. Fray Mier would have been nothing more than a colorful freak if he had not attained grandeur through suffering and through his faith in the destiny of his country.

We can easily picture him in his final years: withered, broken, turned to parchment, but still fiery, still taking part in discussions with that silver-toned voice noted by his contemporaries; surrounded by the gratitude of a nation, and attended—in the palace —with universal love and understanding, godfather of liberty, and the people's friend. And it may be that, in a moment of senile confusion, he would feel himself a captive in the presidential mansion and, led by his bird's instinct, would flit from window to window, peering out to measure the distance to the ground, if he should need to take flight again. Perhaps he entertained the amiable General Victoria, in the president's hours of relaxation, with theological foolery and piquant reminiscence.

III: THE SPIRIT OF THE LEGEND

The heresy, or whatever it was, that Fray Servando was guilty of amounted to a pawky interweaving of two Mexican legends. To explain this, we must look back several centuries.

The Spanish conquistador girded himself for the conquest of America as a soldier of Christ. To him, the theoretical reason for the Conquest—whatever the practical reason—was the same as the reason for the crusades. The soundest spiritual title that Spain possessed to her colonies was the preaching of the Gospel.

And then, in the first century of Spanish rule, the story was bruited throughout New Spain that a miracle had been wrought: a miracle which Our Lady of Guadalupe had designed for Mexico alone, and not for any other nation. The Virgin of Guadalupe had appeared to the Indian Juan Diego, and her image had been stamped on the Indian's mantle. From thenceforth the Virgin, dark like an Indian, was to be the Patroness of Mexico. Later on, in 1810, the insurgent armies took the image of the Virgin of Guadalupe for their banner.

There is reason to believe that this tradition, in which many hopes and beliefs are mingled, was launched as a means of catechism, for the purpose of coloring the creed imported from the Old World with national feeling. At any rate, the tradition springs from the rich Mexican sensibility and has flourished vigorously in that soil. It is one of those beautiful legends of Catholicism in flower: the Virgin cultivates a garden for a poor man and appears to him as a luminous dark lady. This legend of the Guadalupana and Juan Diego, in "La arquilla de marfil," by Mariano Silva y Aceves, acquires an ineffable poetic subtlety: the gentle, simple Juan Diego becomes the symbol of a race.

The Indians knew, from their legends of the creation, long before the white man came, that a white and bearded priest named Quetzalcoatl had appeared one day among them and had taught them how to till the earth and given them two or three rules of good conduct. He is one of those solar myths, more or less explicit, with which the primitive mind likes to personify the first efforts at civilization: he is the Cadmus of America. We cannot here go into all the meanings and consequences of this belief— not only spiritual, but visible and tangible consequences as well— in the history of the pre-Hispanic peoples. It is enough to say that the figure of Quetzalcoatl always had a tremendous fascination for them.

IV: FRAY SERVANDO'S HERESY

And it came about, one fine day, that Fray Servando, young professor of philosophy at the time, with a great reputation as a preacher, set off a bombshell. He was to preach at a ceremony dedicated to Our Lady of Guadalupe. And what did he do? He betrayed his preoccupation with the cause of independence;

through one of those transferences of thought so common in the genesis of our national ideas, he arrived at some bizarre statements which, though they may seem to us laughable, in that day were utterly shocking. In truth, to all appearances the speech was a last-minute improvisation, turned out in an effort to be original, at the suggestion of some friend. And yet it was the cause of all Fray Servando's misfortunes.

The Virgin of Guadalupe—said Fray Servando—was an object of devotion in Mexico long before the Conquest. St. Thomas the Apostle, who was none other than Quetzalcoatl himself, had preached the Gospel in Mexico before the Spanish conquistadors ever did. The image of the Virgin was not stamped on the mantle of the Indian Juan Diego, but on St. Thomas's mantle.

The Archbishop Nuñez de Haro, perceiving what was hidden beneath these statements, ordered sermons to be preached in which the young theologian was denounced by name. Later he was imprisoned. He escaped. He was put back in prison. Again he escaped. And so on and so on, for the rest of his life.

To his persecutors we owe the memoirs of his travels in Europe, one of the most curious and percipient chapters in the literature of the Americas. Let us follow him to the places where his destiny has tolled him. We may catch, here and there, a whimsical glimpse of Europe in the early nineteenth century, or a satirical sketch of a Spain now remote, which will offend no one, but divert us for a time from the vexing problems of our own day.

V: AN EXILE

In the year 1795, Fray Servando Teresa de Mier, now more than thirty, landed at Cádiz, banished from New Spain for a crime that was not a crime, a heresy that was no heresy.

Fray Servando was a Mexican-born Spaniard of noble lineage. Like Mexico's other noble creole (Don Juan Ruiz de Alarcón, in the seventeenth century); he insisted, while he was in Spain, on being addressed as "Don," and on social privileges as well, pointing out that friars do not renounce their noble birth nor their rights as noblemen, and that the Apostle St. Paul proclaimed his rank at every step, despite the arrests and affronts to which he was subjected.

In Spain, where his trial was to take place, Fray Mier had to spend six years, divided between prisons and flight, going from town to town, intriguing with scant success, now in the halls of justice, now in the royal palaces, fleeing down the roads, in a day-to-day existence that would have crushed any soul that lacked his gaiety or his fighting spirit. And the ten years of his sentence would have been spent in just the same way, if our friar had not found a great remedy for his ills, namely, to slip over to France with the aid of a Frenchman living in Astorga, who was a priest and a smuggler.

His "Memoirs" are, naturally, full of prejudice, and at times have the quality of caricature. But for this very reason they incisively reveal some of the basic vices of the society in which he lived.

VI: BETWEEN CHALDEANS AND COMENDADORS

Fray Servando was sentenced to be confined in the convent of Las Caldas, on the banks of the Mosaya between Cartes and Buelma, at the foot of a mountain. There were so many rats in his cell, they ate his hat, and he had to sleep with a bed slat in his hand to keep them from eating him alive. But the worst of it was, he was being eaten alive by fools. Those friars who divided their time between Mass and pot, those Chaldeans of Las Caldas, inspired in him the most profound contempt. His least insulting words for them were "idiots" and "mules fit to be tied to plows."

It is worth noting that Fray Servando expected to be rescued through a certain influence that he had at court, even though he had a terrible enemy in the officer charged with the affairs of New Spain, who was named León and behaved like a serpent. When Fray Servando discovered that the Chaldeans were intercepting his letters, he burst through the bars of his cell and sallied forth into the countryside.

Soon a captive again, he was transferred to San Pablo de Burgos, where he arrived with the reputation of a wild man who had made a pact with the devil, and everyone was astonished to see him so refined, so pleasant, so cultured. Burgos treated him more hospitably than it had ever treated El Cid, for two of the friar's cousins had been abbesses of the noble monastery of Las

Huelgas, where the Knights of Calatrava professed their vows. Hence, the comendadors began to pay him visits, and he found himself in good society.

Nevertheless, the summers at Burgos last only from St. James's day to St. Anne's, and the rigors of winter began to undermine Fray Servando's health. He then asked to be transferred to a warmer climate, in a petition set forth with a good deal of vehemence. And the sinister León replied, from the court, with a recommendation to eat less pepper.

VII: BETWEEN CAVE-DWELLERS AND CRAVATS

"I did not know"—cries the victim of persecution with pardonable bitterness—"I did not know that the real kings of Spain were the 'cave dwellers' in the secretary of state's office."

Fray Servando, with no compass to guide him, had chosen, in taking his case to the royal court, the worst of two possible courses. There were two routes for American affairs: the Council of Indies, and the "restricted" route through the secretary of state's office, which was supposed to be a direct way to appeal to the king, and consisted in merely delivering oneself up to the mercy of the clerks in the secretary's office—the "cave dwellers." All petitions went to them, and they dictated what should be done in each case with four tiny lines scribbled on the margin (or six, when they made a special effort); and the secretary had nothing to do but tell the king what these tiny lines said. Within five minutes Charles IV would get bored, and finally would yawn: "That's enough," which meant: "Dispatch the whole business in accordance with the cave dwellers' advice." And the orders that went out were in strict accordance. As when an order was sent to Havana for a cavalry assault on the English who had landed in Campeche, or when instructions were received on the isle of Santo Domingo to arrest the "comején" (an insect), which had destroyed certain documents requested by His Majesty.

But is there no direct way to reach the king? Indeed there is. The monarch can be surprised as he steps into his coach. The monarch listens benevolently. Then, in his bell-like tones, he says, "Very good." And turns the matter over to whom? Why, to the cave dwellers.

When a cave dweller began to lose his efficiency he was buried in the Council of Indies, and henceforth was called a "cravat." The "cravat," who had sons and grandsons, found it harder to get along on his salary than the cave dweller. The reader can surmise what this meant.

Finally, there were agents for the Indies, who most thoroughly bilked the new arrival from the Americas.

Surmounting all these obstacles, Fray Servando managed to snatch the documents from León and place them before the Council.

VIII: BETWEEN SCHOLARS AND DONKEY-DRIVERS

Fray Servando was saying Mass in San Isidro el Real to help pay his expenses. Meanwhile, the Council asked the Academy of History to prepare a report on Fray Servando's case. And he would have us believe that the Academy spent eight consecutive months on his affair, without considering any other matter in any of its sessions.

Since the Academy's report was favorable to his cause, Fray Servando expected he would be permitted to depart in peace. But the sinister León intervened; Fray Servando took refuge in flight; justice caught up with him again, and this time he was imprisoned in San Francisco de Burgos, to the city's consternation. León ordered that he be confined for four more years . . . (oh heavens!) among the Chaldeans. For four hours the poor friar was stretched out in a faint. He came to, escaped, headed toward Madrid, collapsed from fatigue on the road, was picked up by a donkey driver. His friends in Madrid disguised him; because León had sent out a notice that described him as affable and smiling, Fray Servando contrived to make himself ugly and dour, painted some moles on his face, twisted his lips into a sneer on catching sight of the police, crossed his eyes, and, all in all, obeyed to the letter the slogan of the Portuguese army: "Show the enemy a frightful face."

With these precautions, and with a smuggling priest and a mule driver and a false passport, he crossed the French border, in 1801, and reached Bayonne.

How justly he complains of the iniquity of judges!

" 'Go in, pigs!' cried a swineherd in despair; they had milled about for a maddeningly long while, refusing to get in line and enter the gap of their sty.

" 'Go in, go in—like judges into hell!' And they all rushed pell-mell into the gap, some even entering one on top of another."

IX: BETWEEN RABBIS AND HOURIS

Yesterday our man arrived in Bayonne; today he walks casually into a synagogue and hears a rabbi preach. Fray Servando asks permission to debate the sermon publicly, and—of course—devastates his opponent. The rabbis are overcome with enthusiasm; they call him "the wise one"; they order a new suit to be made for him and offer him a beautiful and wealthy young woman in marriage. He does not accept.

And from there he goes to Bordeaux, in the company of two shoemakers who ply their trade and earn their daily bread, while the poor doctor of theology dies of hunger. The reader can witness his tribulations:

"I was still good looking, hence I did not lack for suitors among the young Christian girls, who had no qualms about proposing, and when I objected that I was a priest, they told me this was no obstacle, if only I would renounce my profession. The multitude of priests who contracted matrimony during the Revolution because of the Terror, which forced them to marry, had removed any scruples that might have deterred them. In Bayonne and in the department of Bas Pyrenees as far as Dax, the women are white and pretty, especially the Basque women."

X: THE CHURCH AND THE CENTURY

In Paris, Fray Servando, aided by his friend Simón Rodríguez, opened a school to give classes in Spanish. In his leisure he wrote polemics against the incredulity introduced by Volney. He was assigned to the parish of St. Thomas, but it turned out to be bad business. He had to pay for many frills: a Swiss guard, two cantors in priests' capes, and a musician who gave them the pitch with a bass fiddle shaped like a serpent. So he made nothing out of it, and his profession cramped him in every way: "In France it would be scandalous for any religious to be seen in a theater, or on a public promenade, especially on holidays, or even in a café."

Just the same, Fray Servando is able to give us mundane reports on the cafés of Paris, the splendid libraries, the promenades, the Palais-Royal, the shops for courtesans, the cabarets and the fashions, which, in that day—according to him—permitted each woman to wear the kind of clothes and to arrange her hair in the style that best suited her type and temperament.

But Fray Servando was, in truth, weary of his profession, and he resolved to hang up his frock. And in order to obtain release from his vows he went to Rome, by way of Marseilles, where the girls wear the mantilla, as in Spain. He made the journey almost without expense, for the French were very hospitable, and his presence and conversation were so charming, all who dined with him and heard him talk became his friends. Coming, as he did, from such faraway lands, his prestige was almost that of a mythological character. And he turned this most admirably to his advantage. And still he can say, now and then, with sardonic humor:

"I am not capable of holding grudges. In vain my friends have recommended to me a modicum of Christian villainy."

XI: THE LAST PAGES

How Fray Servando obtained release from his vows; his observations on Rome, on Naples, on Florence, on Genoa; the trials that awaited him before he could return to Spain by way of Barcelona; his satirical descriptions of the regions of Spain that he traversed on foot from Barcelona to Madrid; the populace dressed in Goya's colors; the slovenliness of the Court—these are the things that fill the final pages of the "Memoirs." They cannot be summarized: they demand to be copied in full. For such a novelist as Baroja, for the sensitive critic of Spanish life, these "Memoirs" should be a rich mine.

Mexico in Films:
Eisenstein's Wasted Work

ERGE EISENSTEIN, the world-renowned Russian film director, first became aware of Mexico near the start of his career, when his curiosity was aroused by an assignment to make a picture from one of John Reed's stories with a Mexican setting. Later, while under contract to California companies, he crossed the border and briefly viewed the landscape at the northern frontier town of Tijuana. But what he saw there in no way resembled the land he had conjured up for himself, and he kept on working in Hollywood. The scenario for his film was based on Dreiser's novel, *An American Tragedy;* the producers insisted on the usual mutilations; Eisenstein tore up his agreement with Hollywood and accepted an offer from the government of Japan.

He was about to board ship for Nipponese shores when he got into conversation with the well-known journalist Upton Sinclair —the one who many years before had exposed the slaughterhouses in Chicago, author of *Oil* and other attacks on capitalism—and with the Mexican painter Diego Rivera. The most thrilling and alluring accounts of Mexico were given him by Rivera, who bewitched him with the characteristic wizardry of his talk.

Eisenstein resolved to change his itinerary, and in December,

1930, made his appearance in Mexico. He was guaranteed the necessary funds by Upton Sinclair and his friends. Two cameramen accompanied him everywhere he went, and he selected the actors for all his roles from among the people of the countryside and the mountains, with the single exception of a stenographer, employed in a government office in Mexico City, who suited him for the heroine's part.

His troubles soon started. The group that was subsidizing him saddled a "manager" on him, a relative of Sinclair's with no apparent qualifications for the job, who loathed Mexico and found a thousand ways to interfere with Eisenstein's work. Eisenstein did not give up, however, but stayed with his strenuous task for thirteen months. He studied the history and customs of our people, even to the most isolated patterns of life. He was on intimate terms with the younger generation of Mexican artists and writers and received their help and advice.

His plan called for the simultaneous showing of the film "Viva Mexico!" in Mexico City, Moscow, Paris, and New York. His backgrounds were all natural. There were no lights, other than the sun. There were no sets, no cardboard. He used a technique for sound that produced effects of the utmost naturalness. Voices were heard, but not in wearisome dialogue: in chorus, in murmurs, in cries, as accents to the drama. The photography, surpassing that in Eisenstein's previous efforts, was captivating in its simplicity. The pictures probed the suffering of the people and the ecstasy of the landscape, awing the spectator with the majesty of sky and mountain, fascinating him with the hieratic sadness of Indian faces, solemn and spare of expression. Horsemen rode by like centaurs, ranchmen in huge hats, swathed in their traditional mantles of gaudy stripes, the sarape. Indian women stood in line along colonial aqueducts, water jars on their head, a vision from the Bible. The atmosphere was imbued with a tragic serenity.

Here is a table of scenes:

Prologue: Evocation of the past; its survival in the present.

Episode I: Tehuantepec, life in the tropics. Heat and humidity. Luxuriance of nature. Folklore. Easy-going idealism.

Episode II: "Apotheosis of the Maguey" (the Mexican agave from whose sap pulque is made, sacred to the ancient Indians). Life on a pulque plantation on the plains of Apan, in the state of

Tlaxcala. Snow-capped volcanoes in the distance. The peon's story: his struggle, his toil. The deep melancholy of the countryside. Glorification of the horse. Guitars.

Episode III: "The Fiesta." Religious celebrations. The Virgin of Guadalupe. Market days and popular dances. Colorful customs. Bullfights—five thousand meters filmed with the Mexican matador Liceaga.

Episode IV: "The Revolution." Eisenstein intended the focus, in this scene, to be a woman, a camp follower or *soldadera*, through whose soul the tragedy of civil war would be reflected. Background: the cactus desert of Tehuacan, one of the most desolate landscapes in the world. The authorities had offered assistance in the form of trains, artillery, troops, and other elements needed to simulate the forces of Villa and Zapata, the chieftains with greatest following among the country folk. The filming of this episode was never completed.

Epilogue: The new Mexico, whose restlessness is not to be concealed, but which is oriented at last in its ideals.

Eisenstein took all his filmed material to Laredo, and in that frontier town was forced to wait nearly two months for a permit to reënter the United States. From there he embarked for Russia, where previous commitments called him. He left his rolls of film in Sinclair's hands. Sinclair tried in vain to sell them; he even went to the desperate and deplorable length of trying to sell them piecemeal. The capitalists of the concern appointed three experts who enjoyed their confidence. And these have mutilated and patched the artist's magnificent work according to their lights. The Mexican epic has been chopped into a series of incoherent scenes which give a very poor idea of the country's life, and which no doubt will be exhibited under Eisenstein's name. It is to be feared that the most earnest effort the modern art of the cinema has made so far to interpret Spanish America has collapsed in dismal failure. The Mexicans who contributed their knowledge and counsel have sounded the alarm. The worst of it is that mystery veils Eisenstein's present whereabouts: no word of him has reached Mexico.

Rousseau Le Douanier
in Mexico

THE CURIOSITY that drew Guillaume Apollinaire to seek
out the bizarre must have been richly rewarded by his discovery
of Rousseau Le Douanier, and in a double sense: for this was not
only a pictorial find, it was also a picturesque find. And among
the possible picturesque episodes of that life, what could be better
than a voyage to Mexico on military service—"as a musician with
his regiment," Adolphe Basler specifies—back in the days when
Napoleon III intervened with his army? An old article by Apollinaire, dated in 1914 and included in the book *Il y a* (Paris,
Messein, 1925), contains several passing references to the prob-
lematic sojourn in Mexico, where critics have sought to find the
source of two or three canvases by Rousseau.

> Tu te souviens, Rousseau, du paysage aztèque,
> Des forêts où poussaient la mangue et l'ananas,
> Des singes répandant tout le sang des pastèques,
> Et du blond empereur qu'on fusilla là-bas.

(The last line seems to allude to Manet rather than to Rousseau.)
Paul Morand recognized, or thought he recognized, familiar
canvases all along the road from Vera Cruz to Mexico City.

"Yes indeed," he says, "the only things missing in the scenery

143

here are the recumbent gray Negro, the lions whose manes have been curled with tweezers, the small tricolored flags, and the pot-hooked signature of Rousseau himself."

I realize that it is truly painful for some of us to forego our colorful little fictions. And yet, it is better to know the truth. Roch Grey, in his booklet on Henri Rousseau (Rome, Valori Plastici, 1922, page 19) writes as follows:

"It is believed that he took part, as a young man, in the war in Mexico, and that his virgin jungles, apes, tigers, sorcerers, flowers suggested by the lotus, the groves of palms, the orchids, are all recollections of the days he spent in the service of his regiment. Is it possible that he would have let his memories fade under the dusty mantle of time, under the gray monotony of his life in Paris? . . . These exotic paintings, as fresh in their youthful fancy as his heart itself, did not appear until the last years of his old age, toward 1904, six years before his death. Is it credible that he would have retained all these memories, without making any use of them, for forty years? Moreover, the flora of Mexico does not in the least resemble the wonderful things in these paintings. . . ."

We might add to these remarks the point that our customs-house officer could easily have found his inspiration for the paintings in certain cheap sets of natural history illustrated in color—the one by Buffon, among others. At any rate, whoever knows or discovers the facts should make them public.

1930

Diego Rivera
Discovers Painting

WHEN DIEGO RIVERA was a child they would dress him up in a black suit on Sundays and special occasions. One day the boy placed his hand on a freshly whitewashed wall and then pressed the hand against his chest. The prints of his palm and five fingers were there for all the world to see.

"What have you done?" his aunt shrieked. "White on black! How well that goes!"

The phrase, and the thought too, stuck in the boy's mind, and for several days he went about chanting to himself:

"White on white does not go. Black on black does not go. White on black, how well that goes!"

Along about the beginning of the first European war, Diego told me this anecdote, assuring me that this was how he got his first idea of painting.

"And the second?"

"The second? When I noticed that the laundress, to make the clothes whiter, tinted them with blue, put indigo in them."

. . . Je suis contraint, assez ineptement, d'en tirer quelque matière de propos universel . . . Montaigne, I, xxvi.

(. . . I am driven, rather absurdly, to draw conclusions that have universal applications . . .)

145

TABLE OF CONTENTS

AUTUMN

WINTER